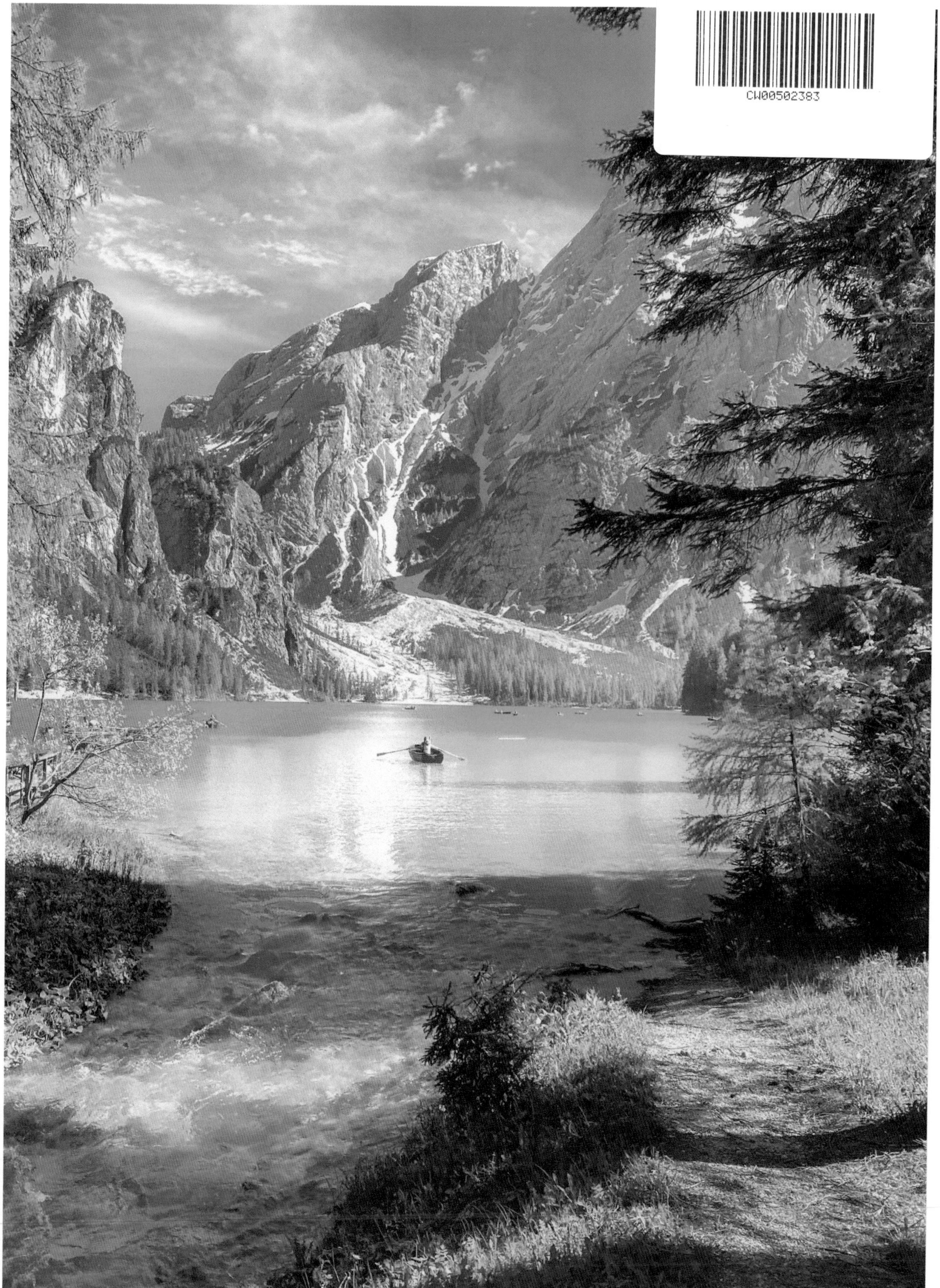

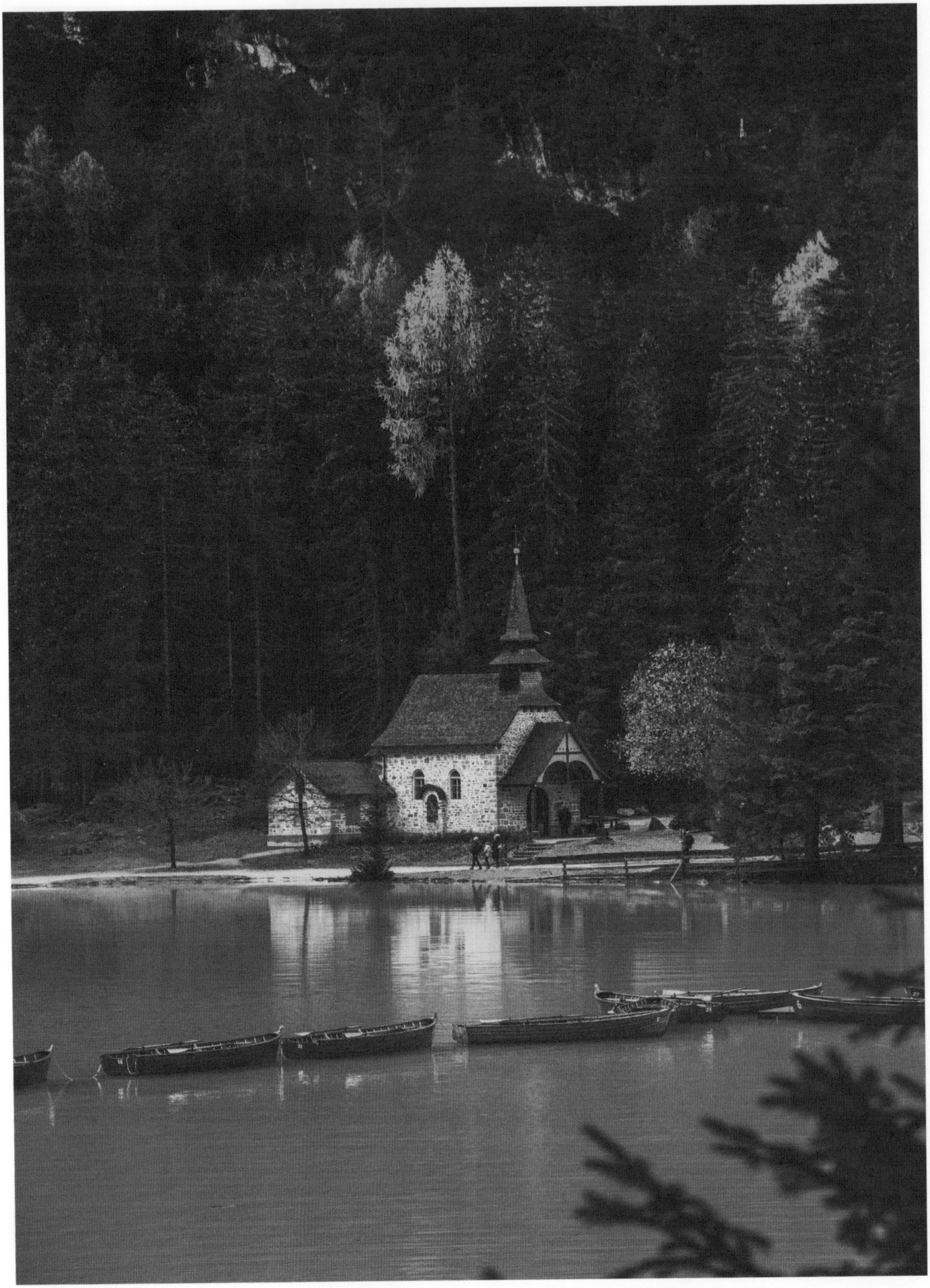

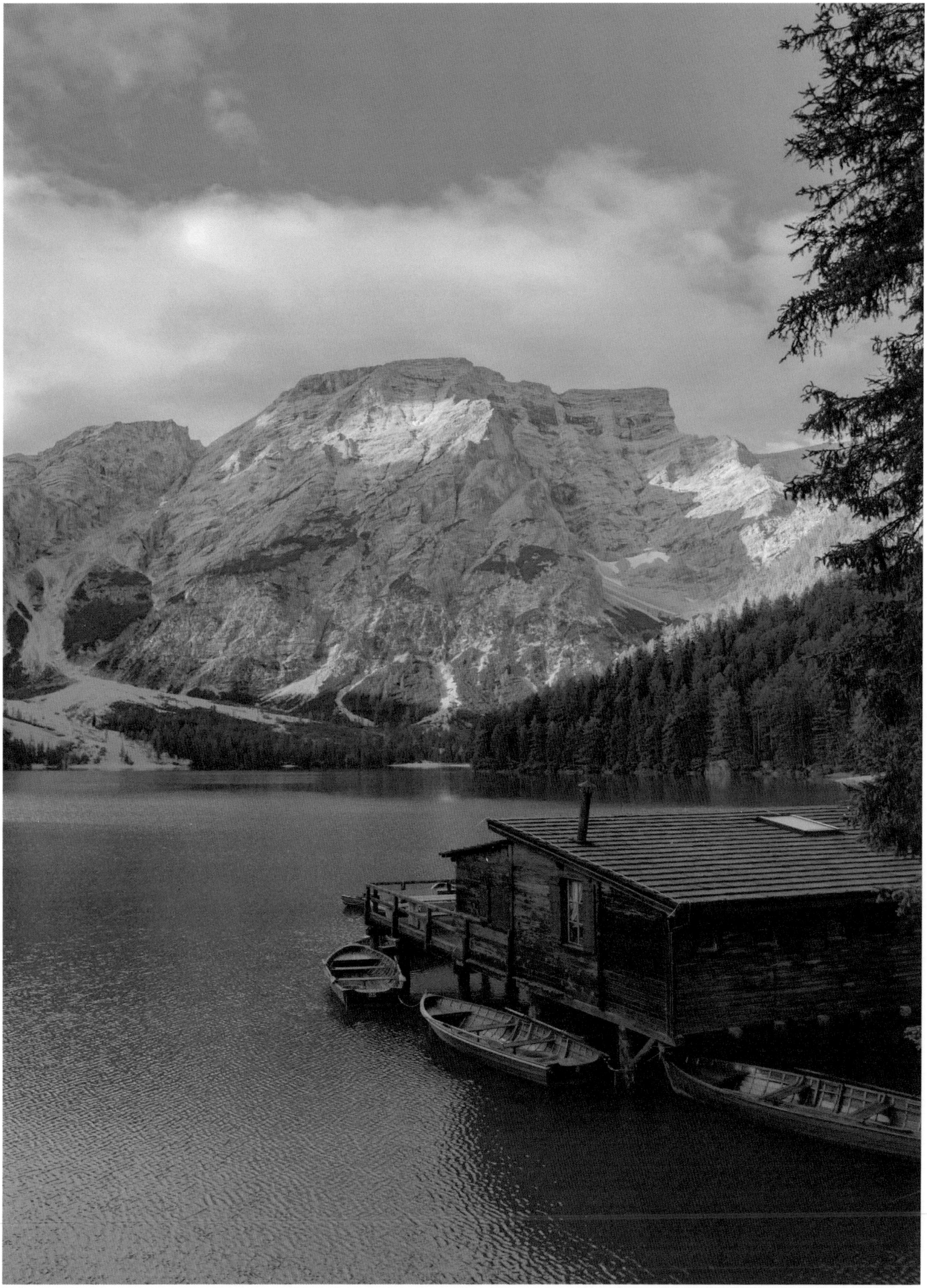

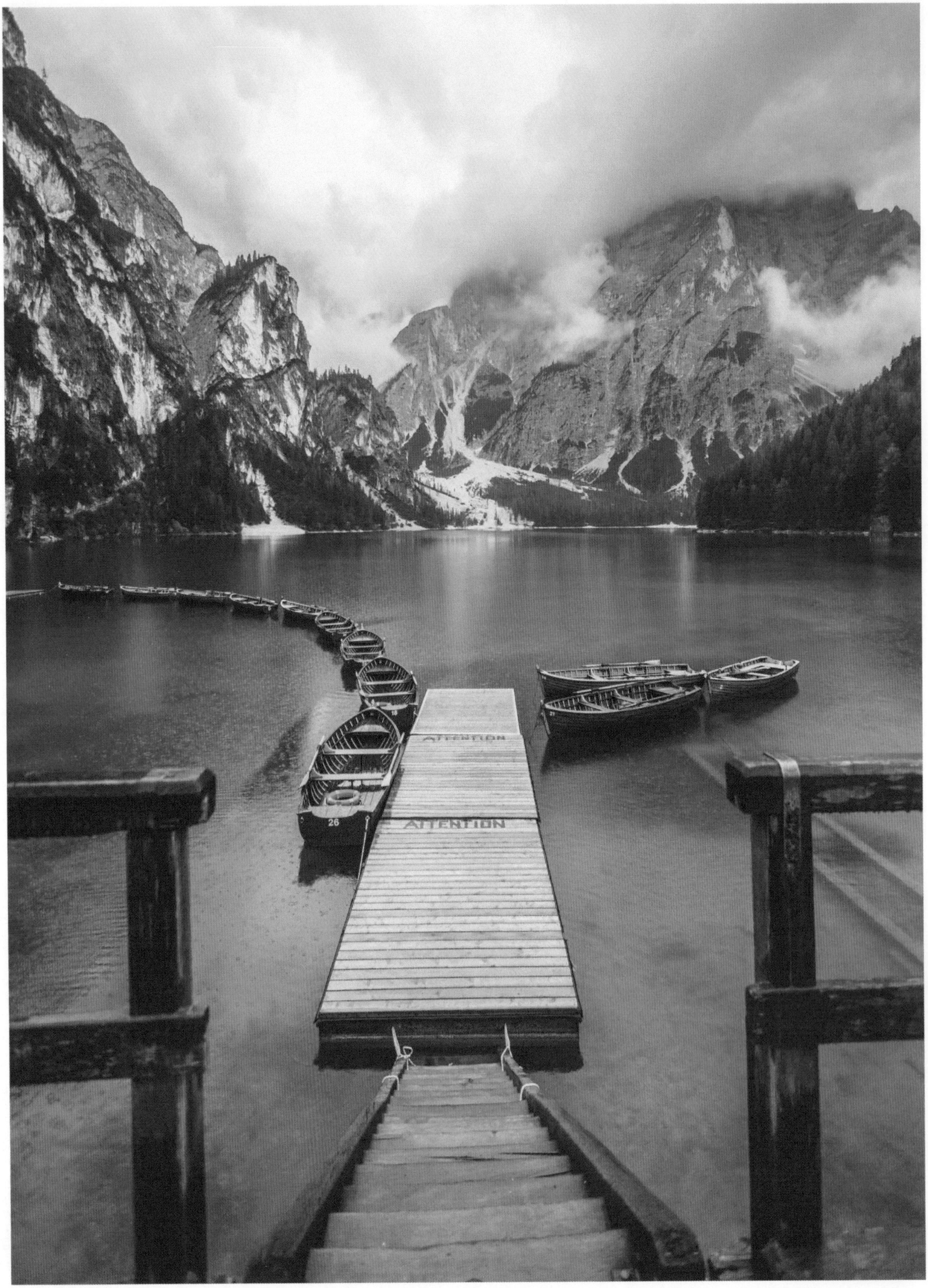
ATTENTION
ATTENTION
26

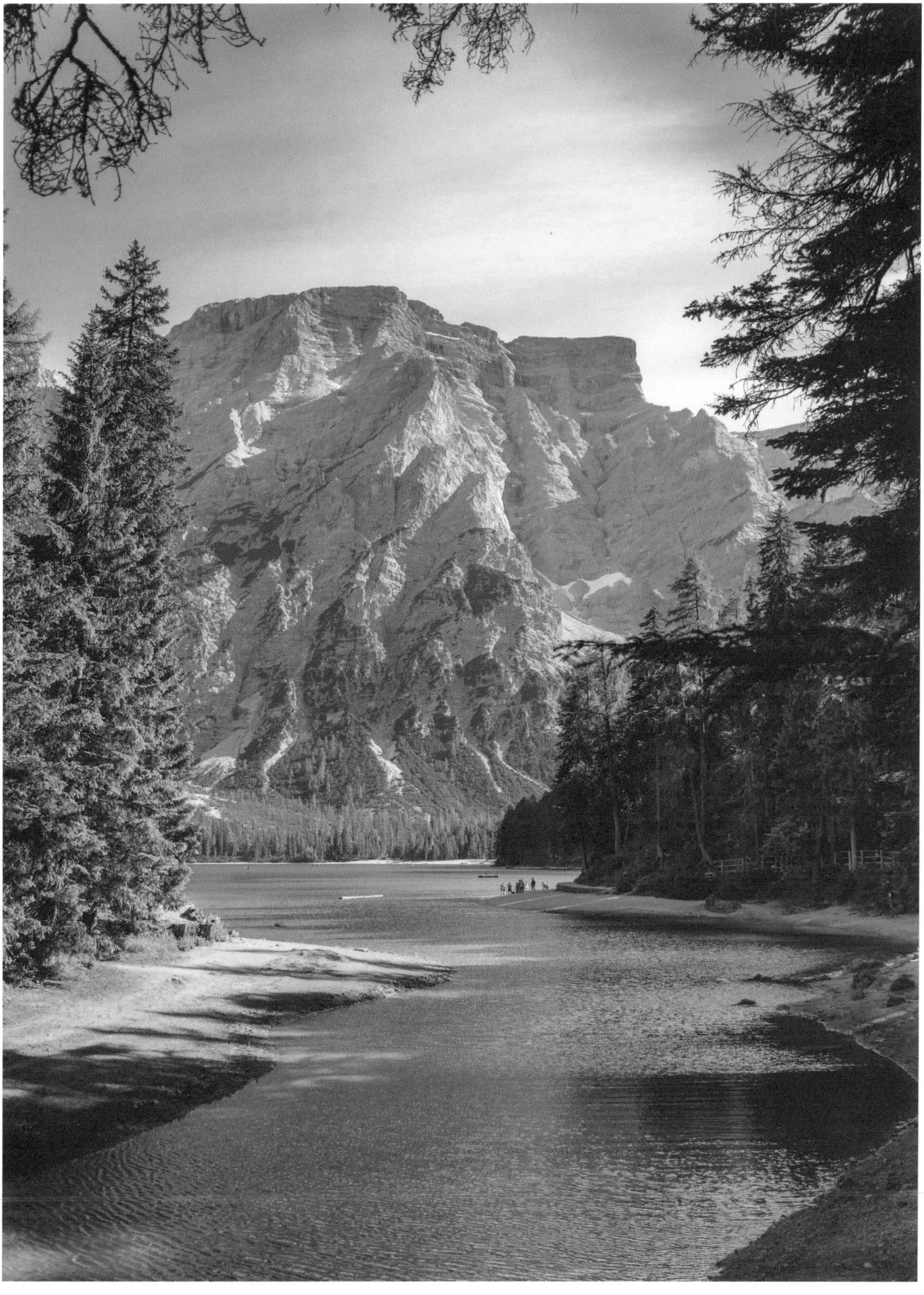

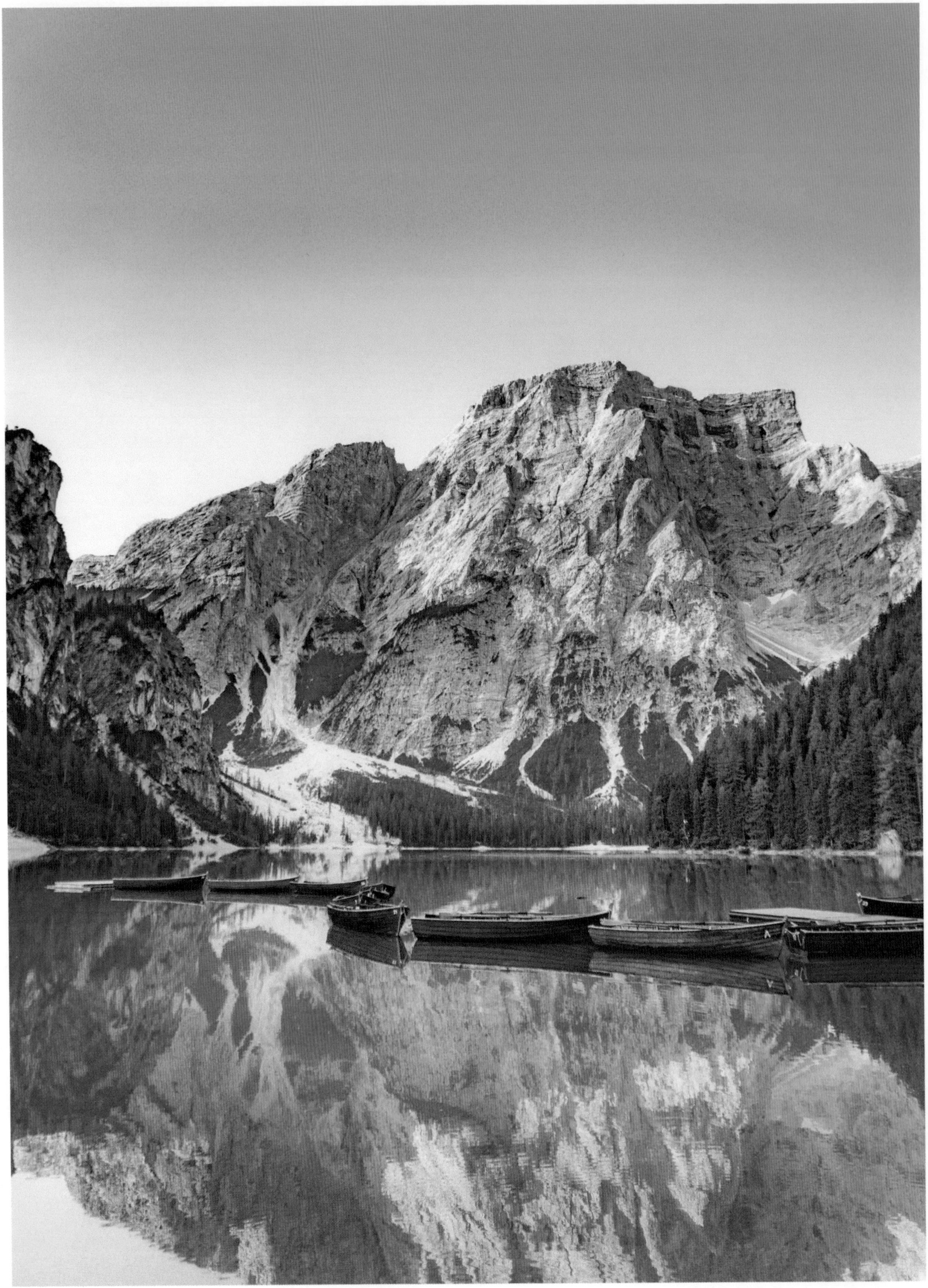

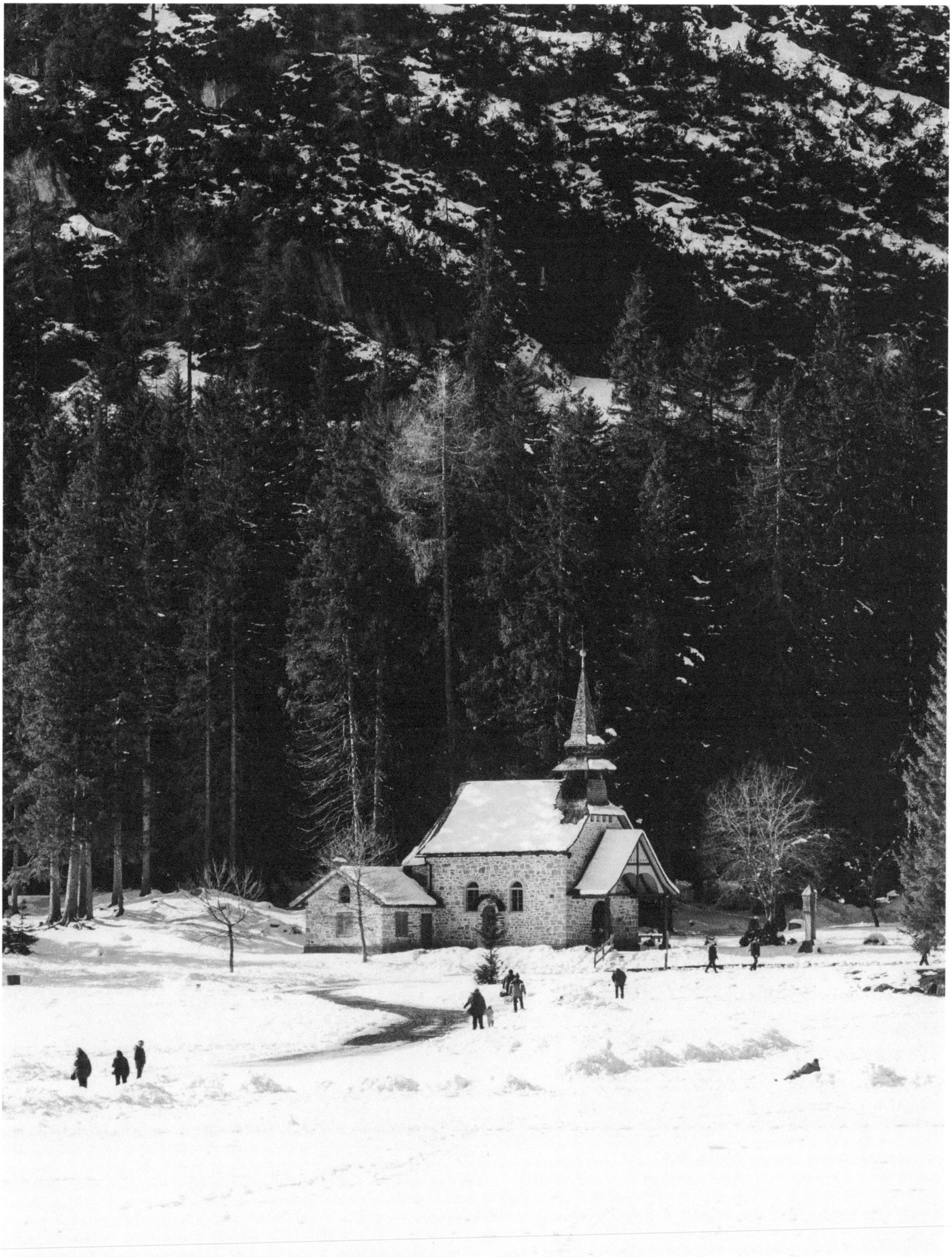

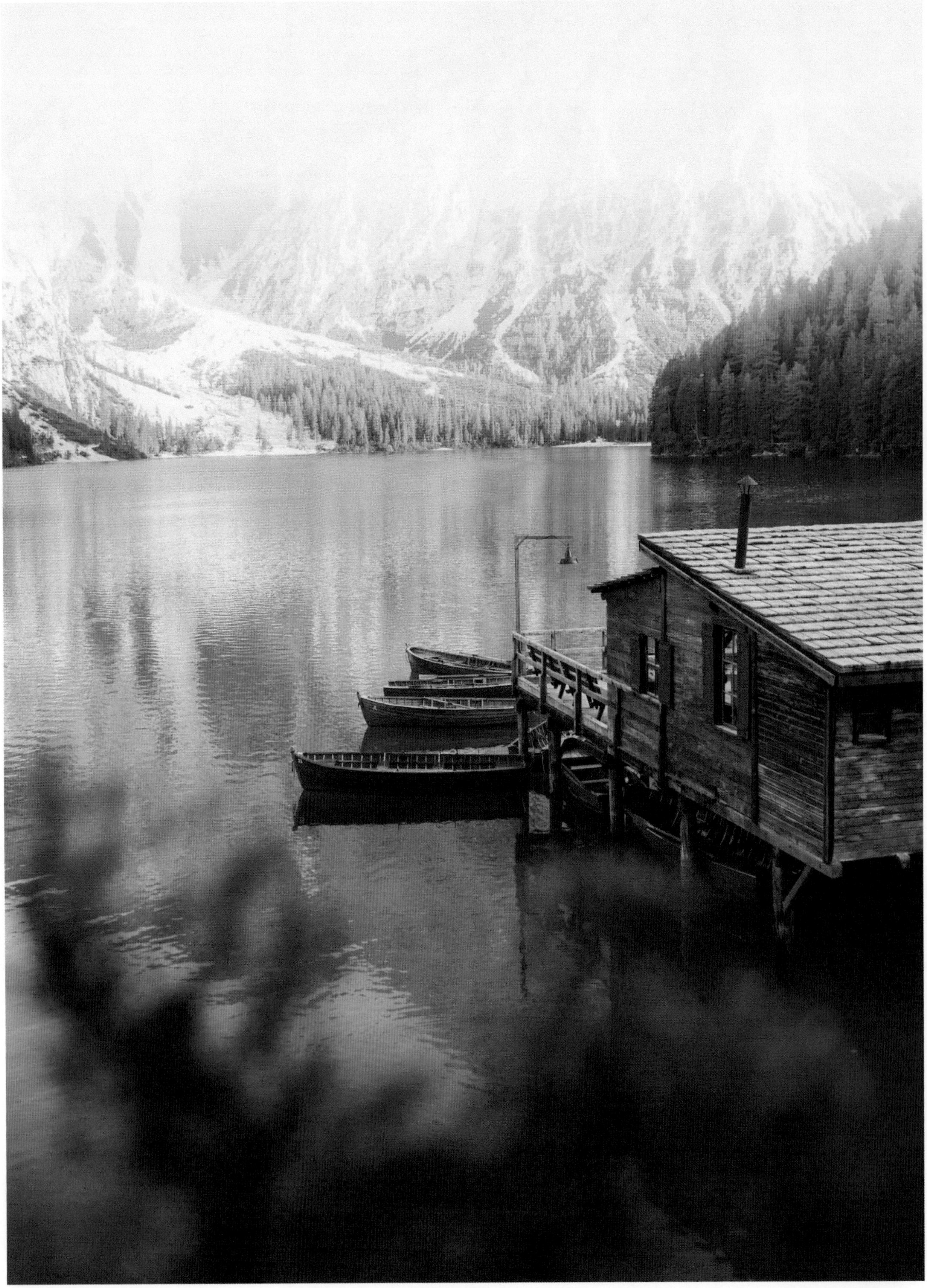

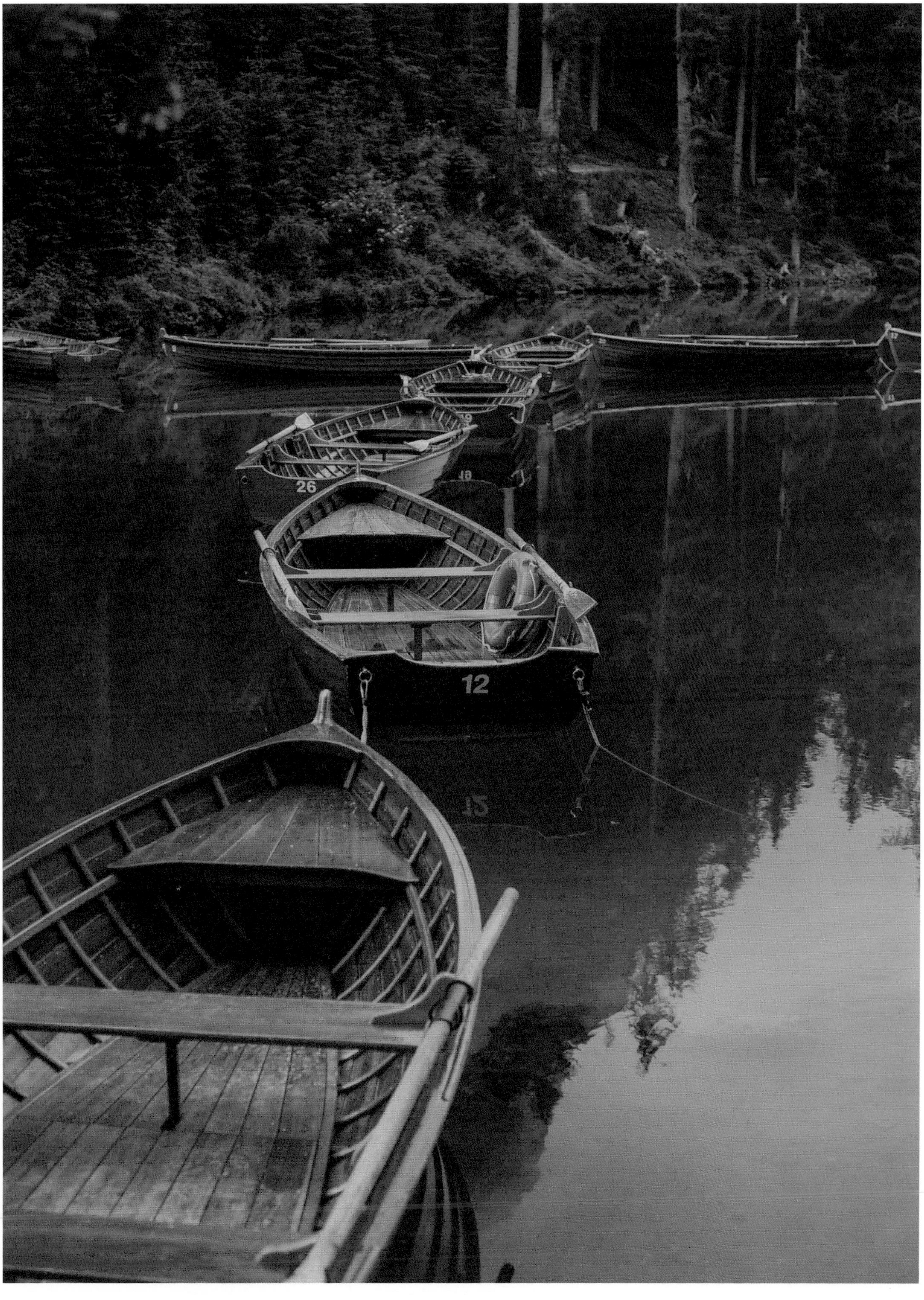
26
12

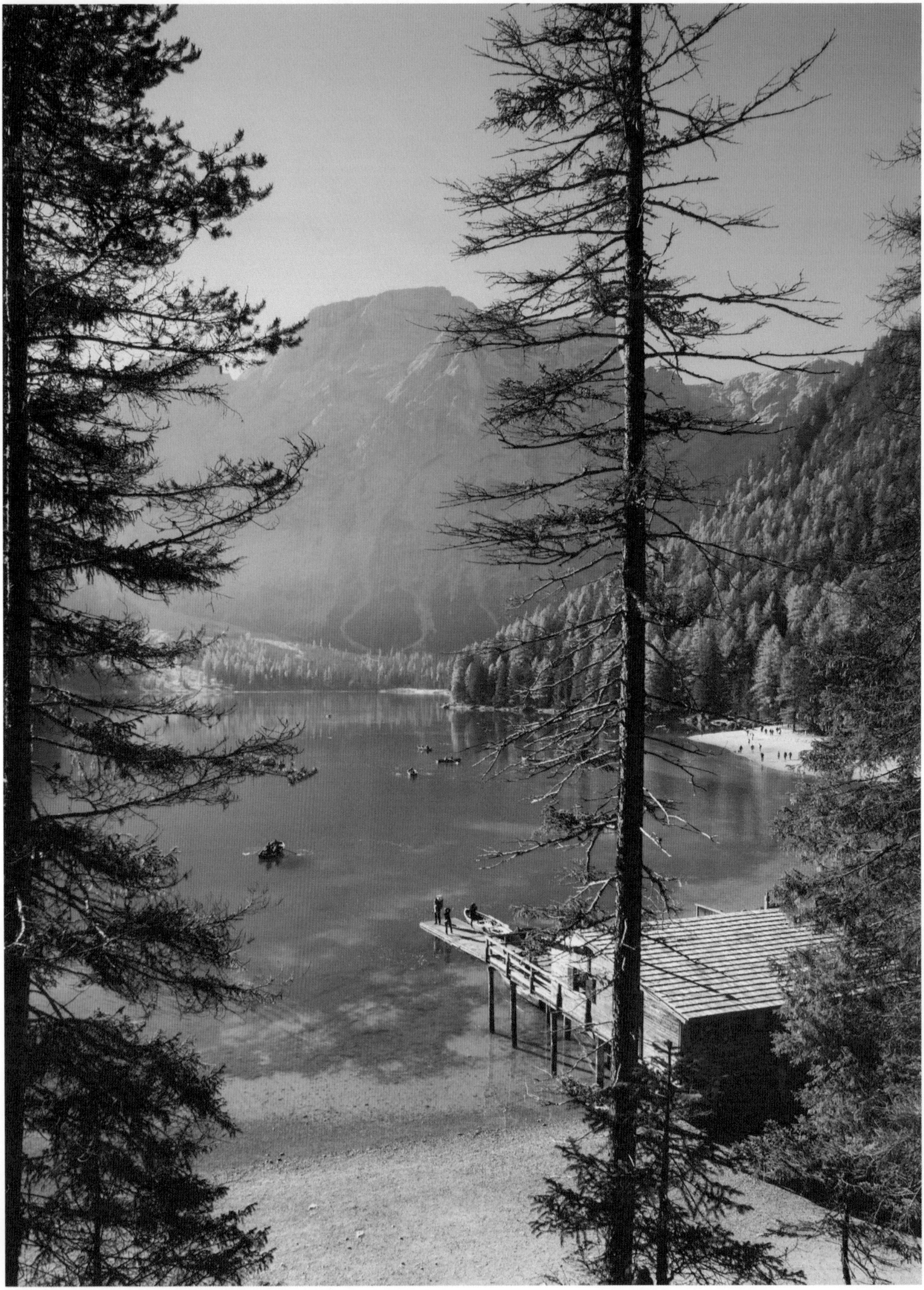

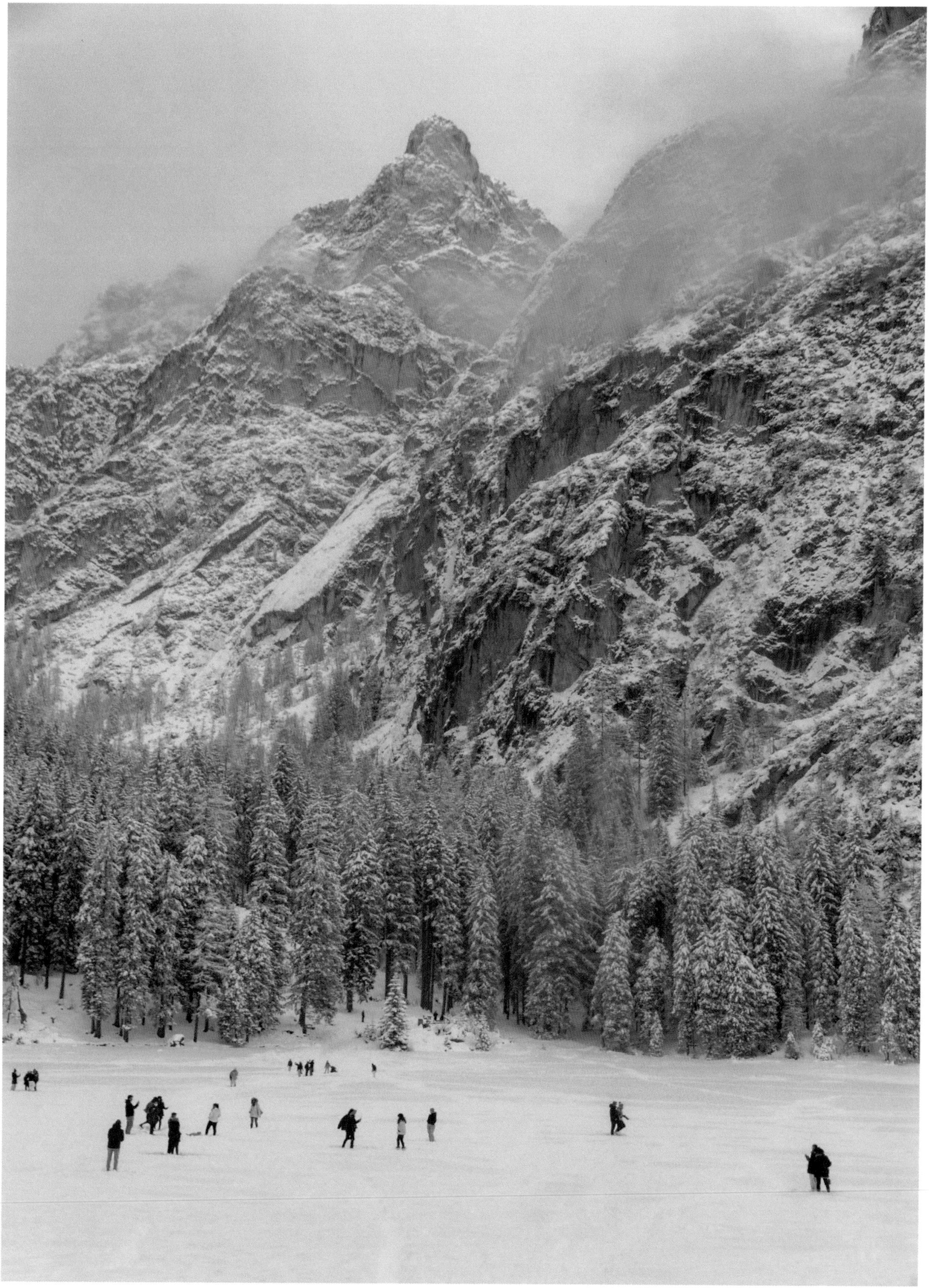

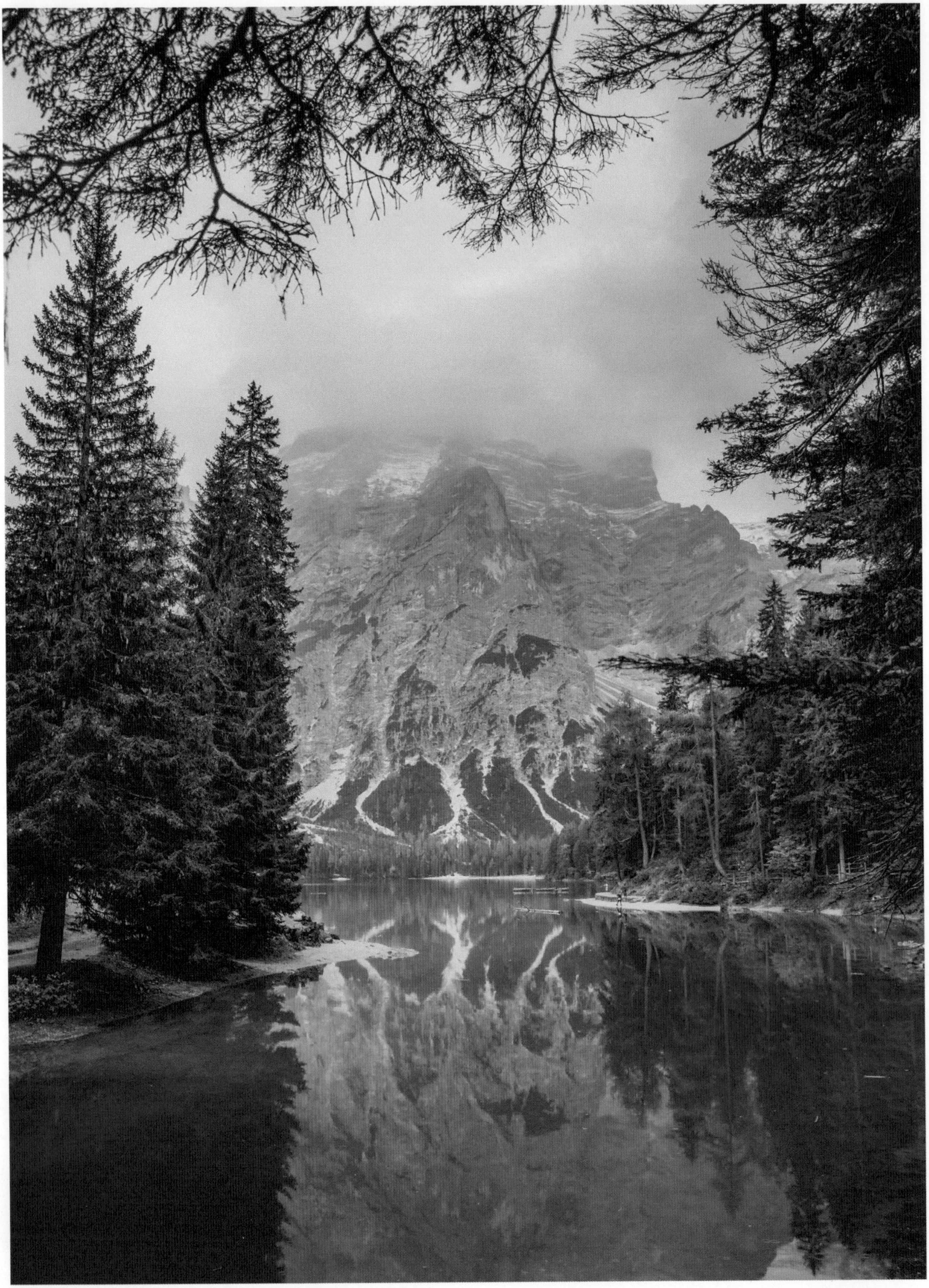

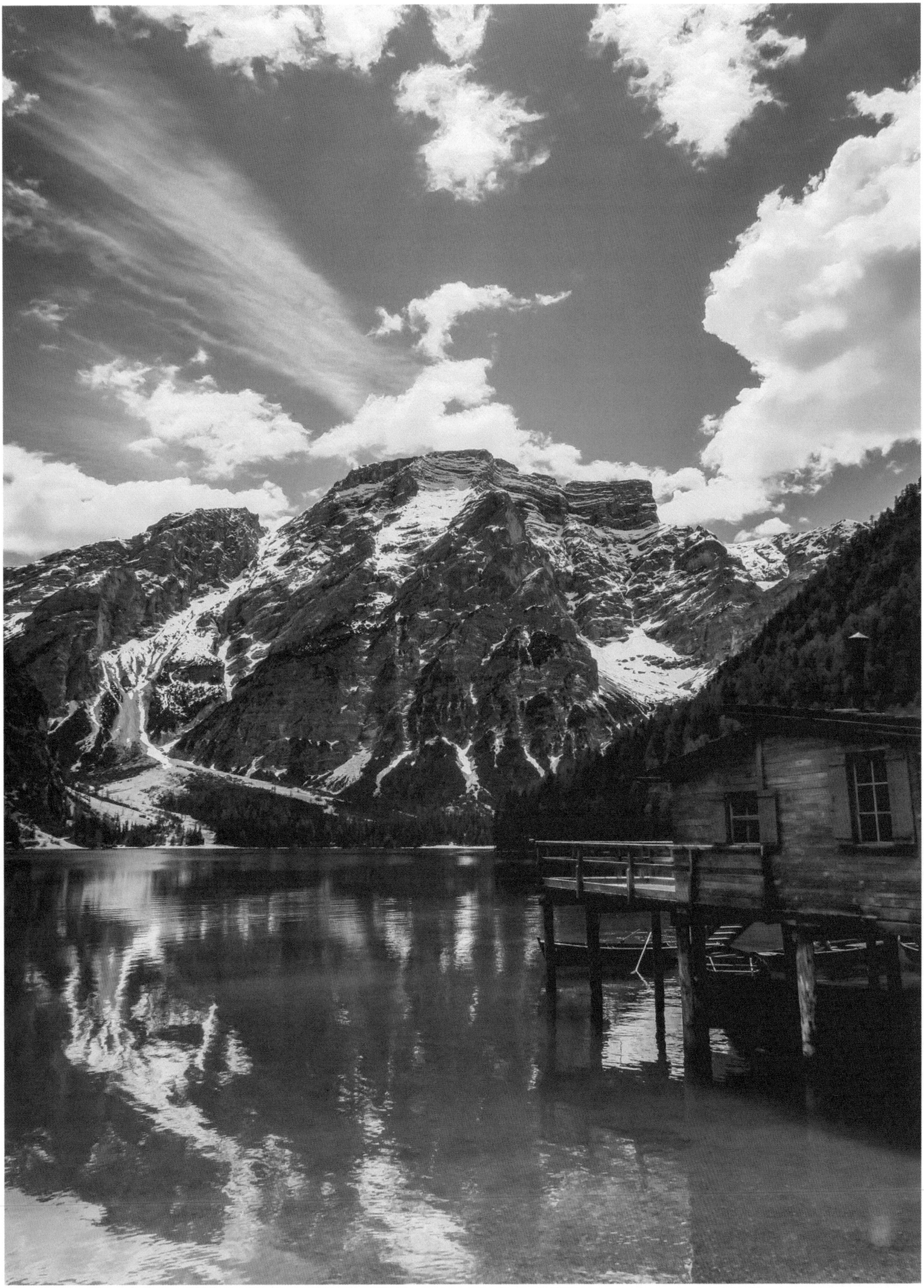

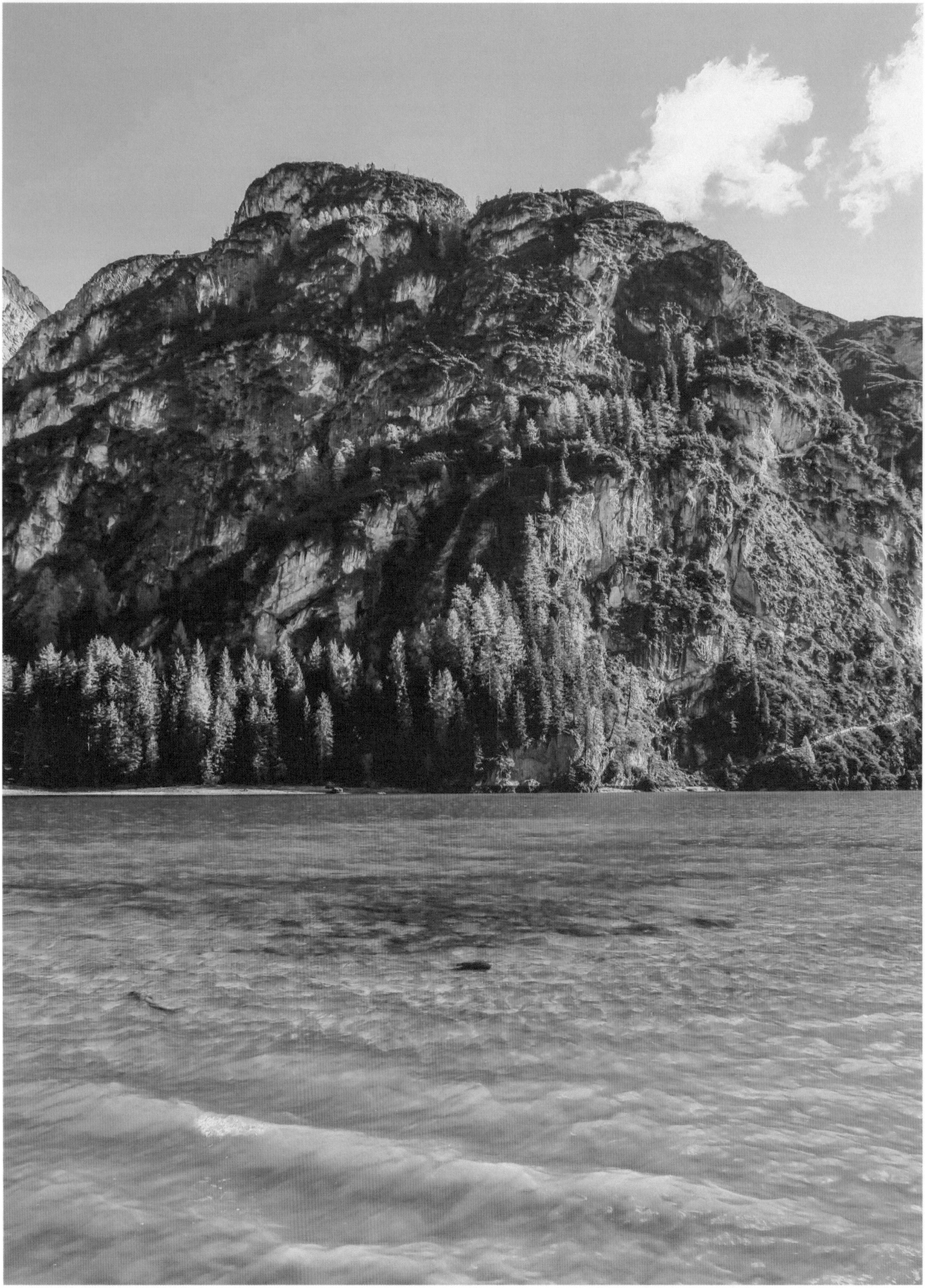

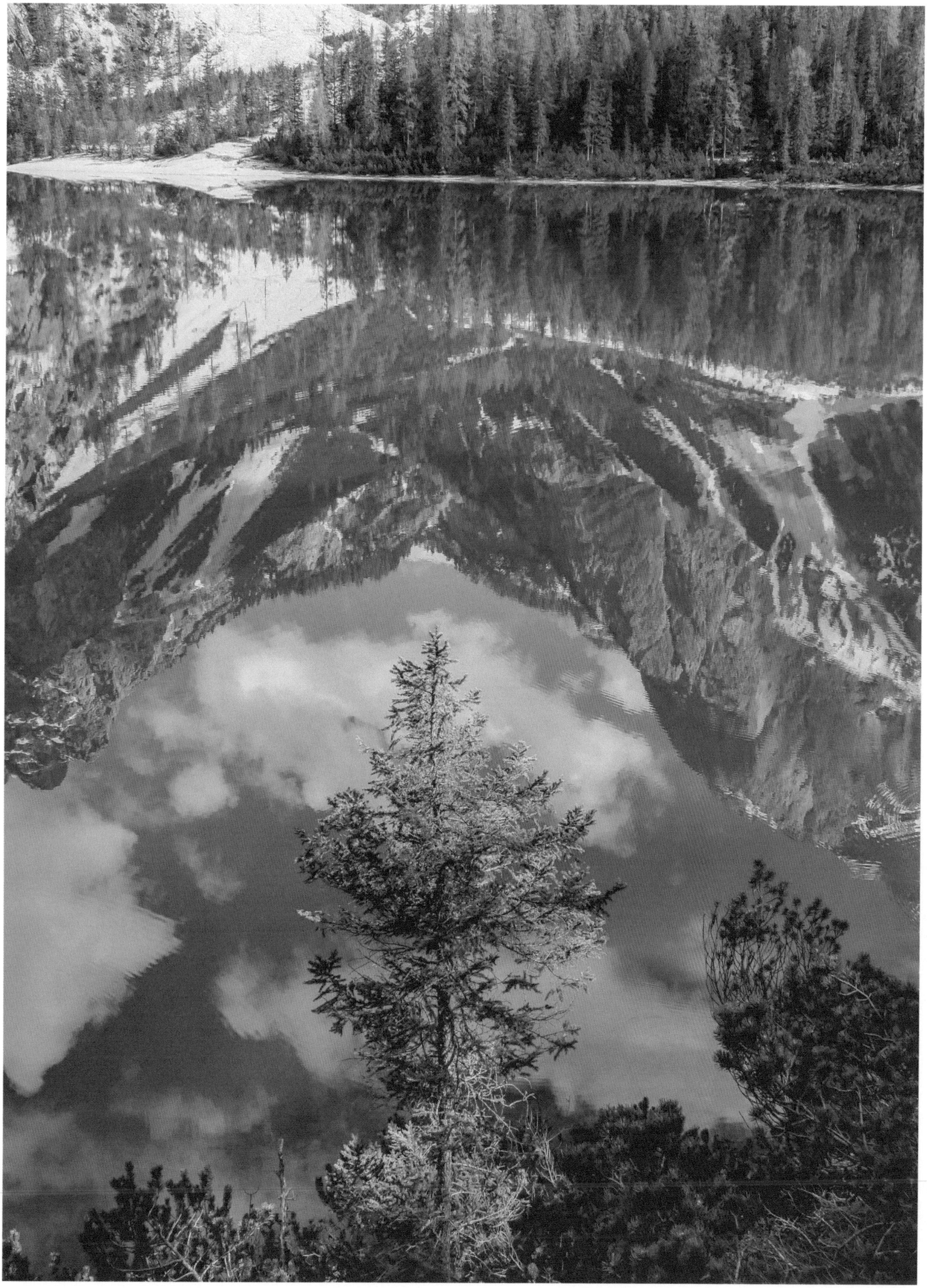

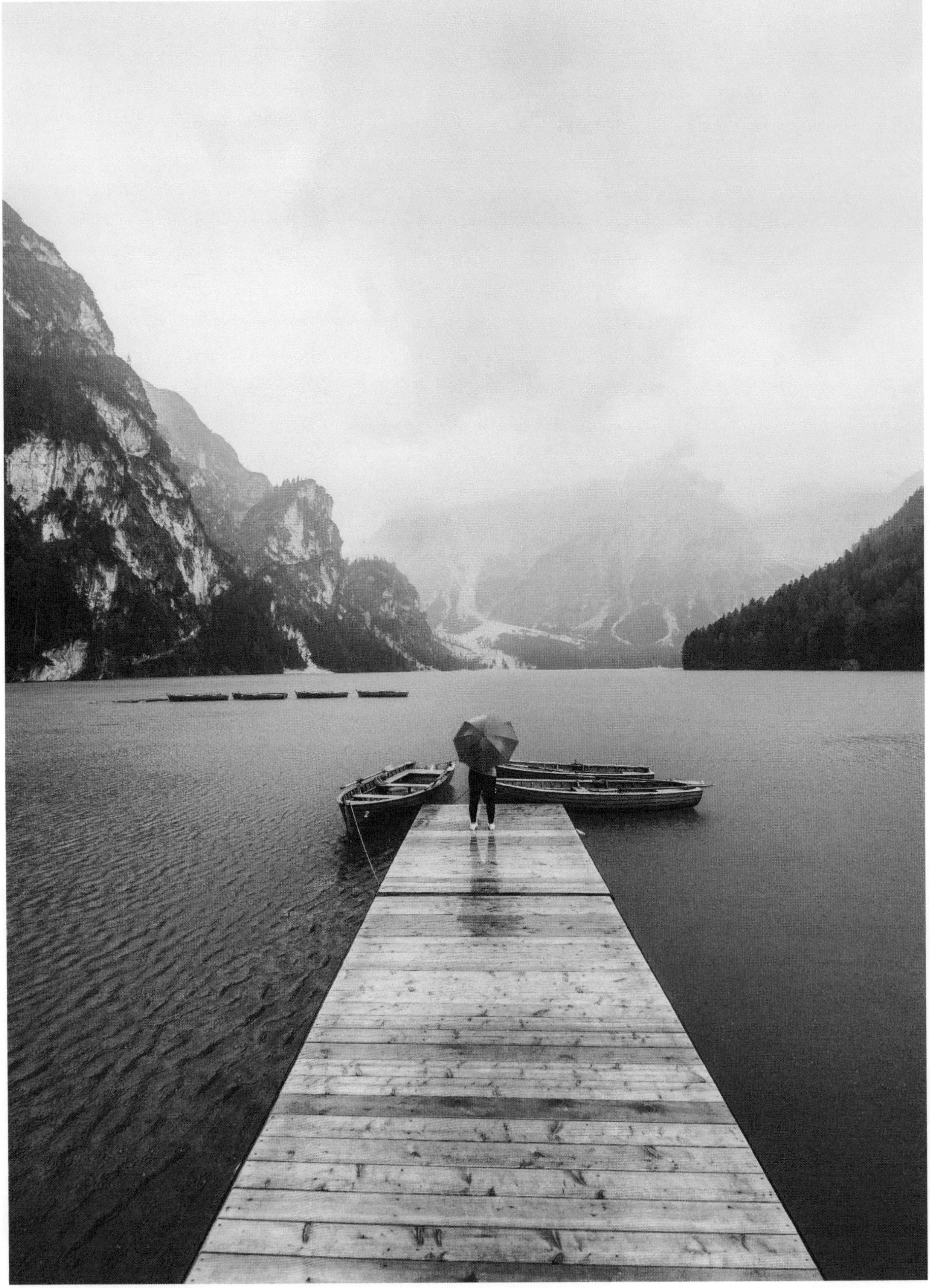

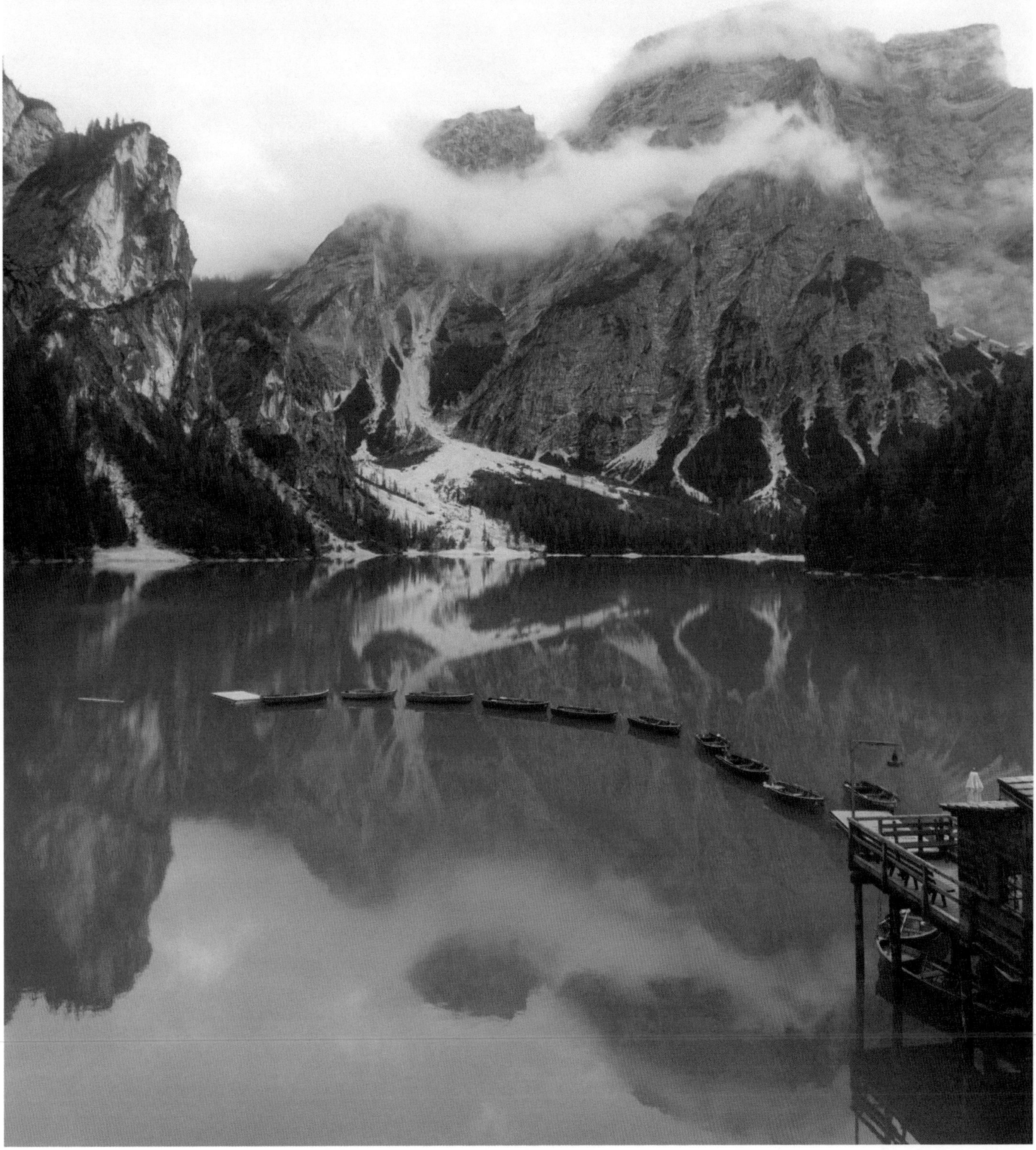

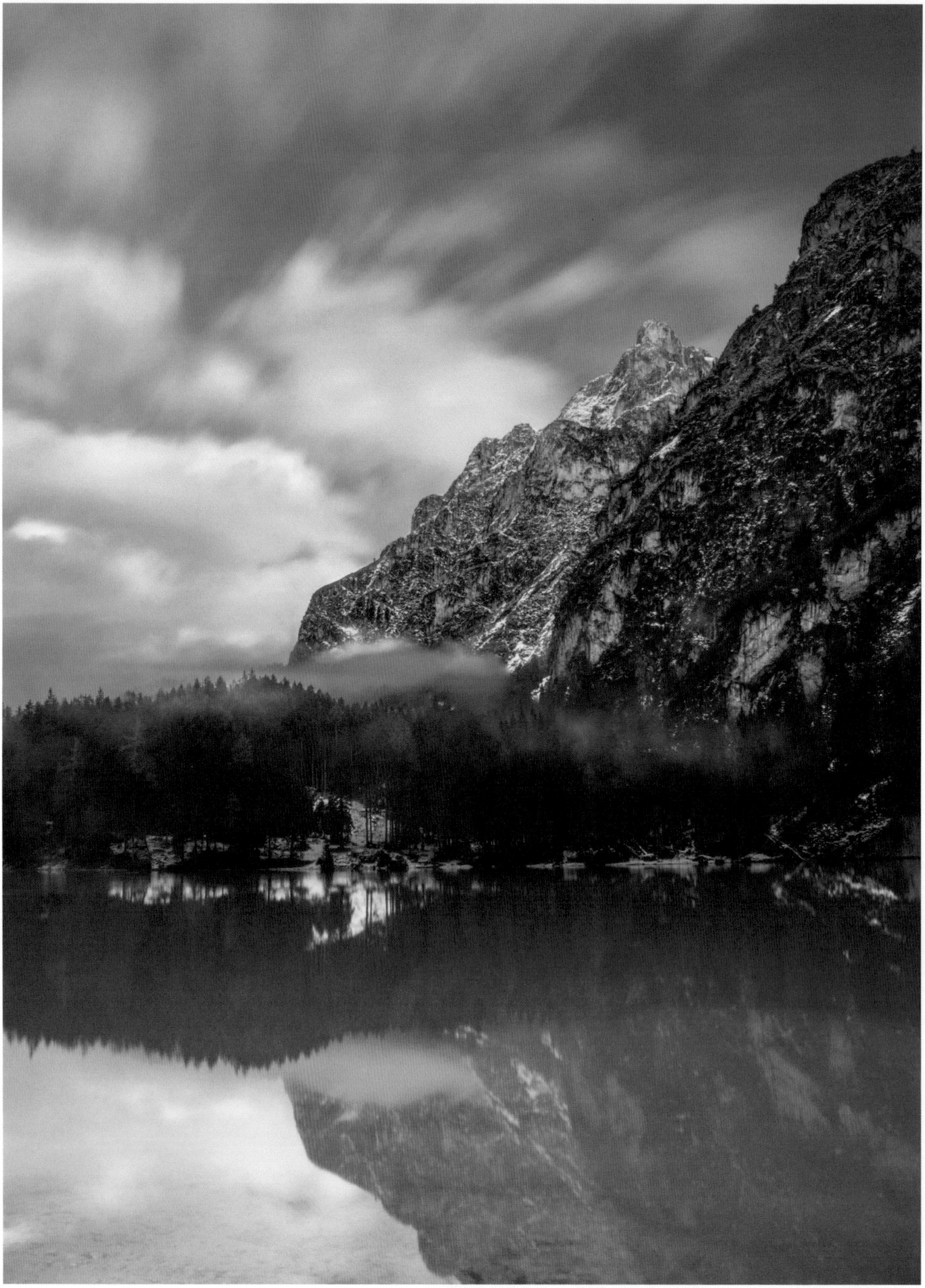

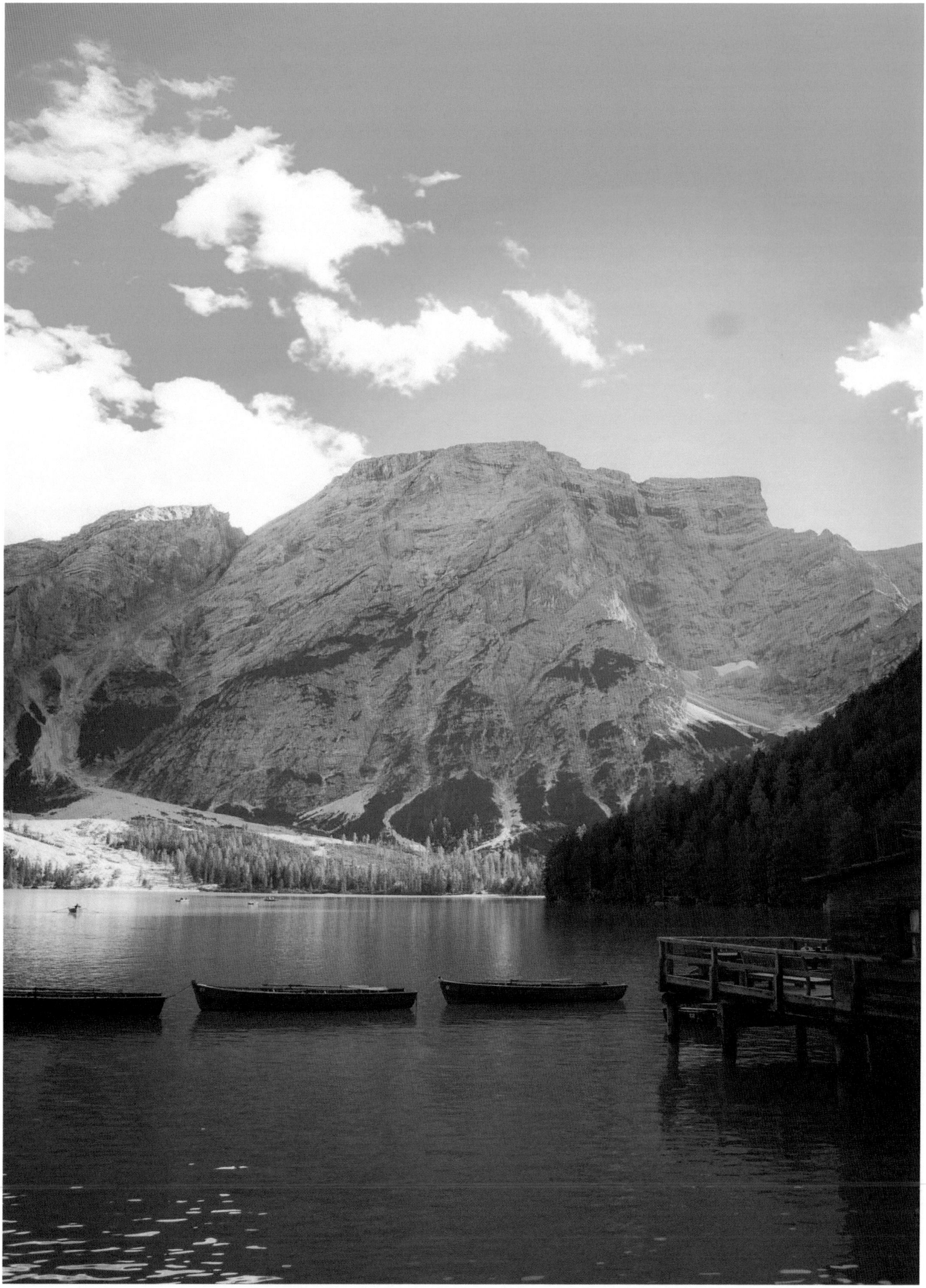

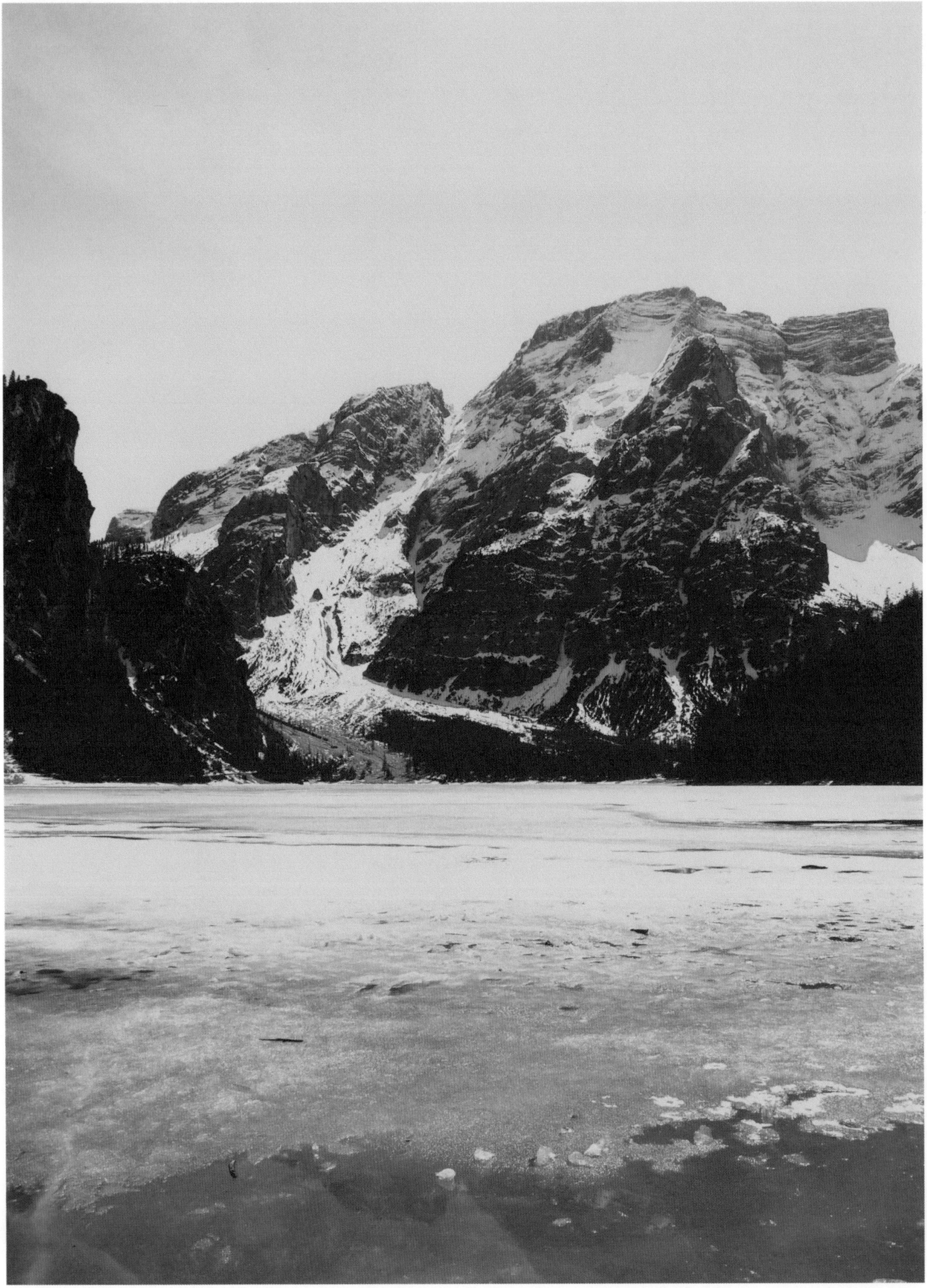

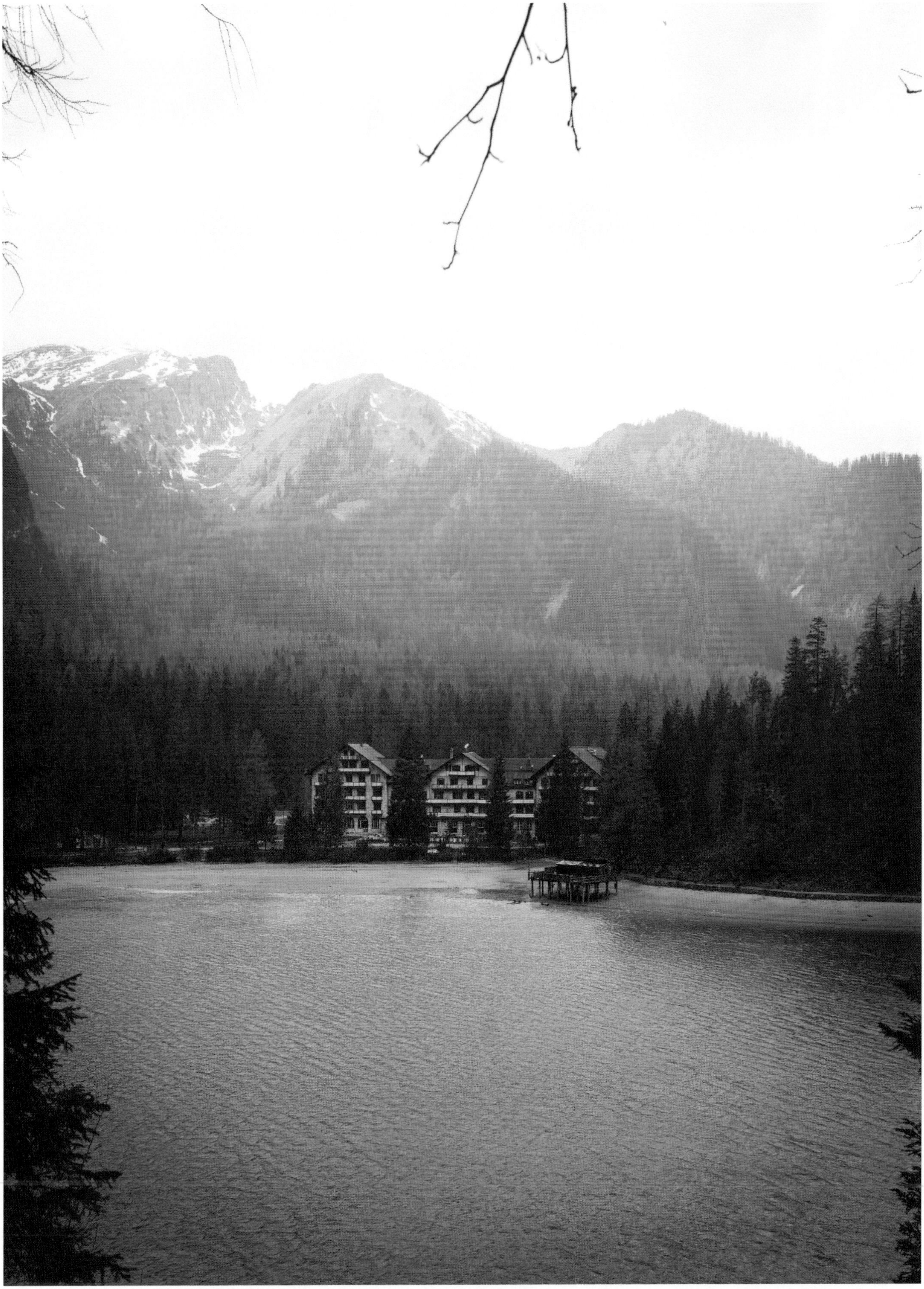

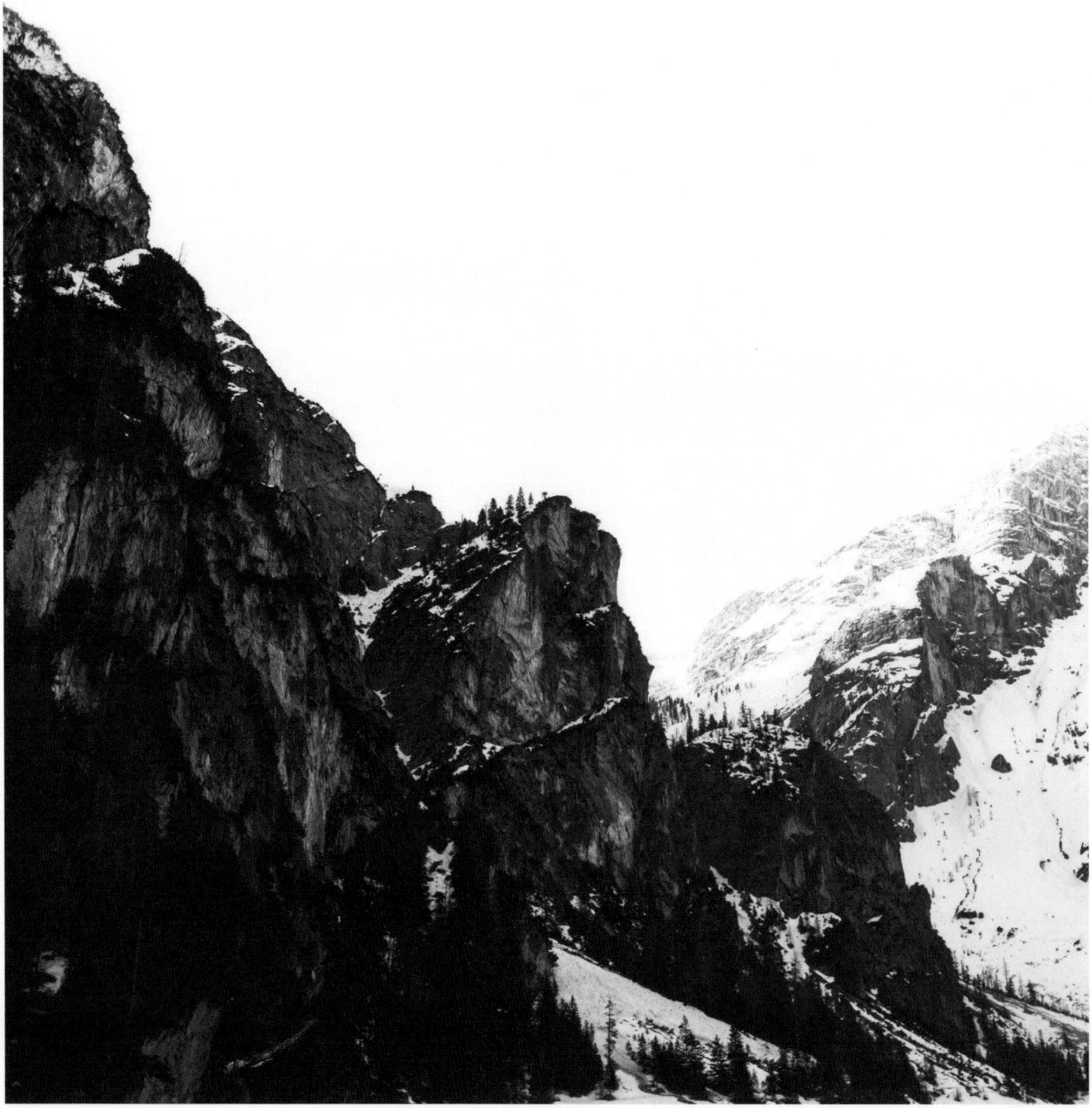

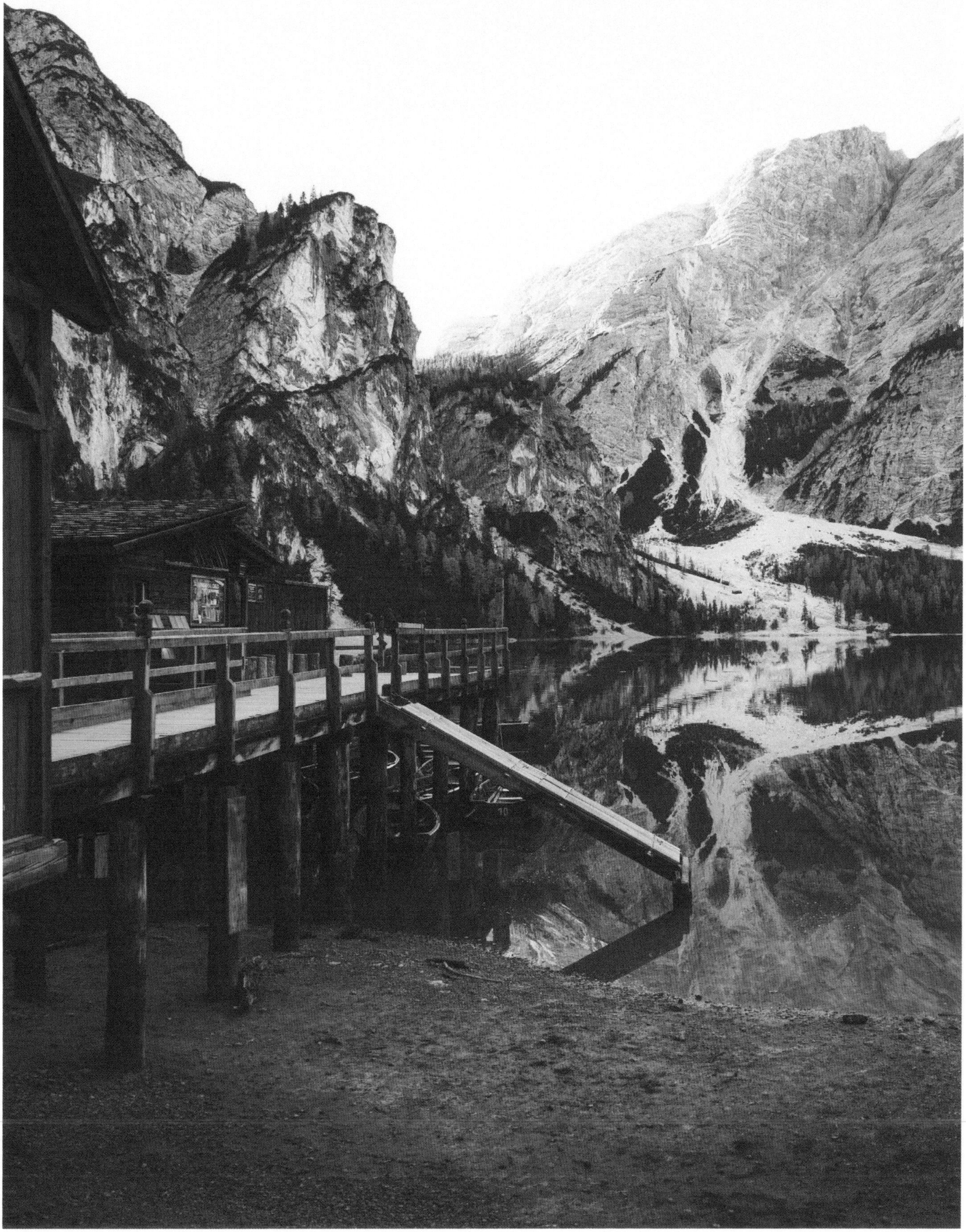

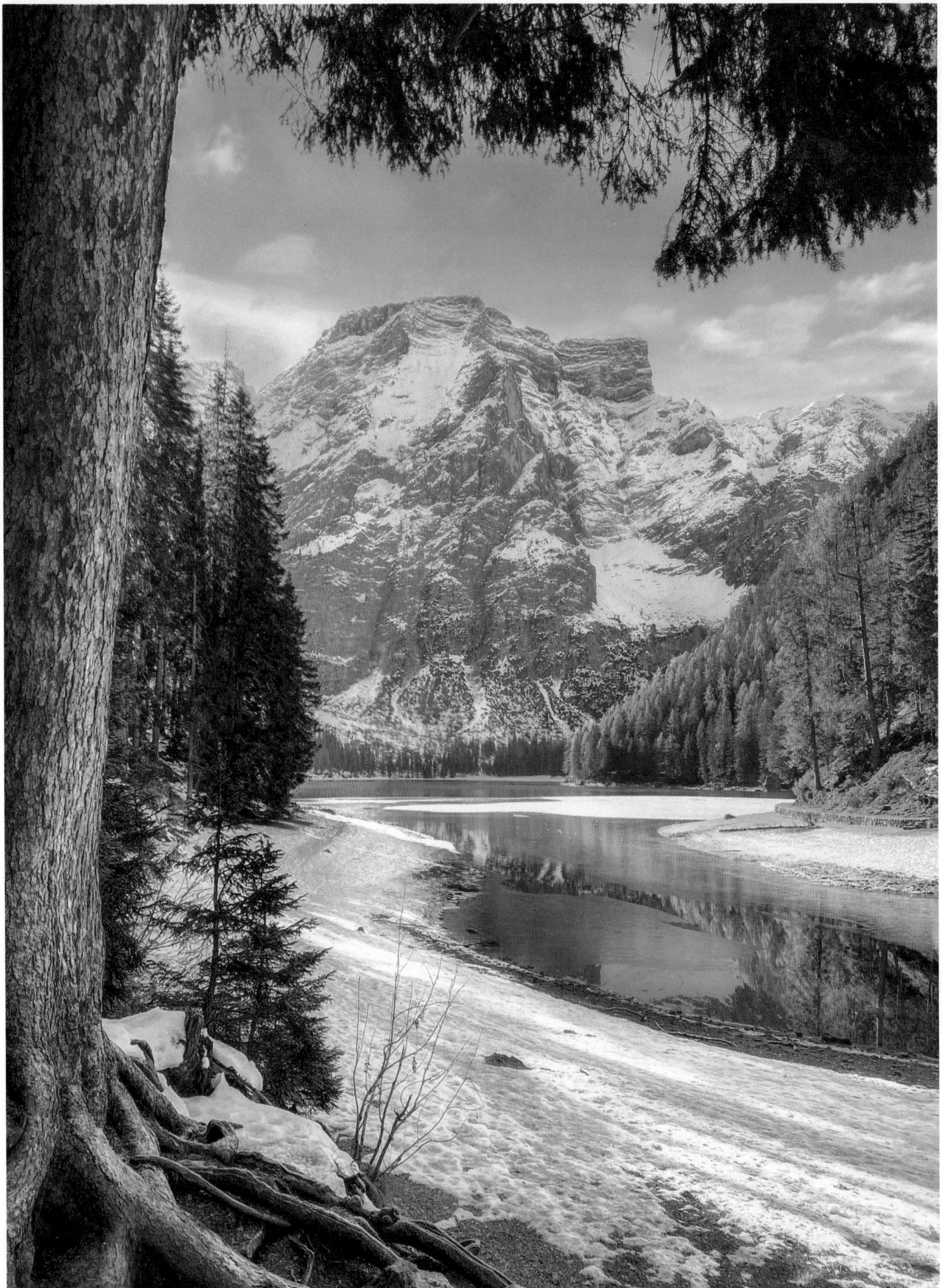

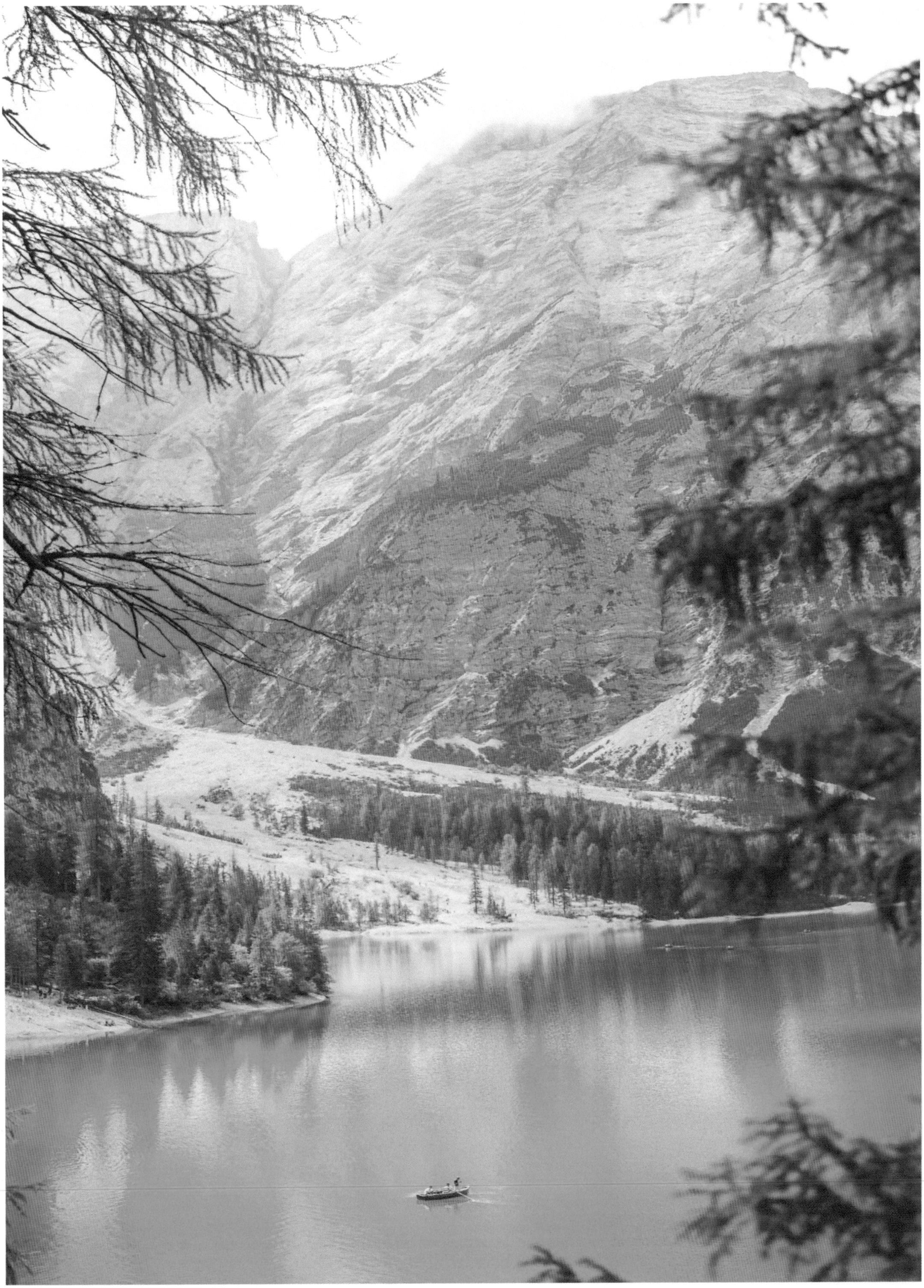

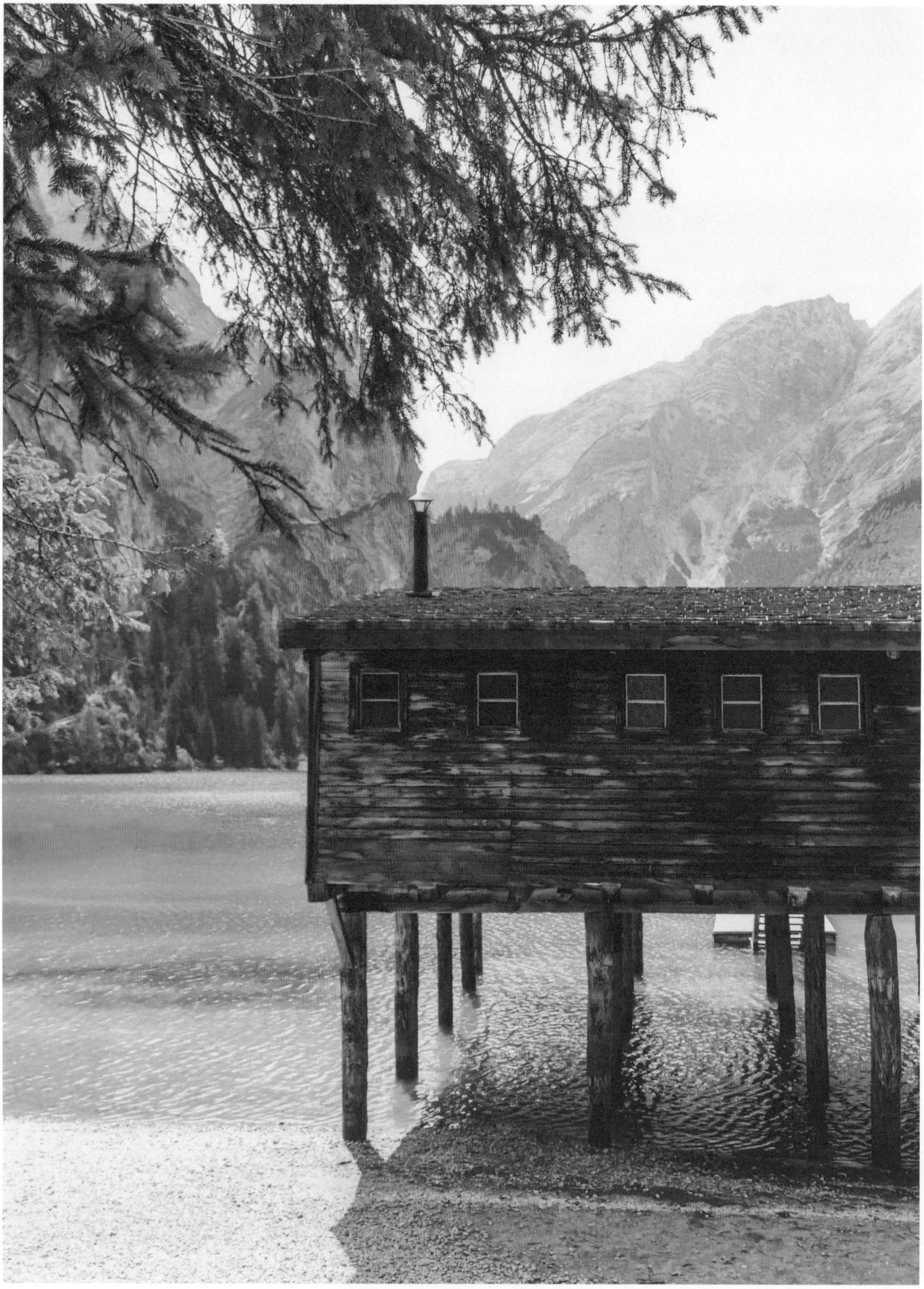

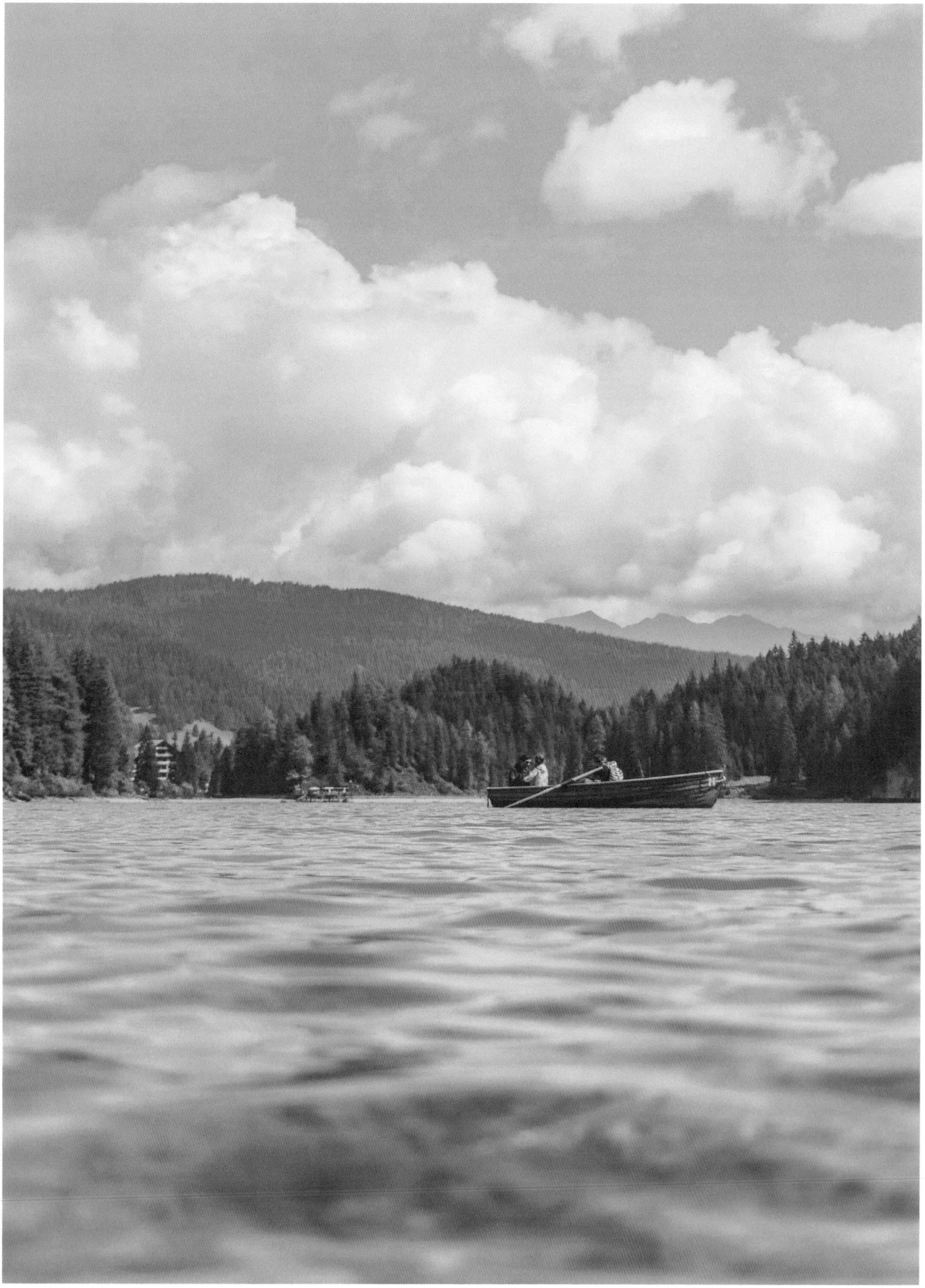

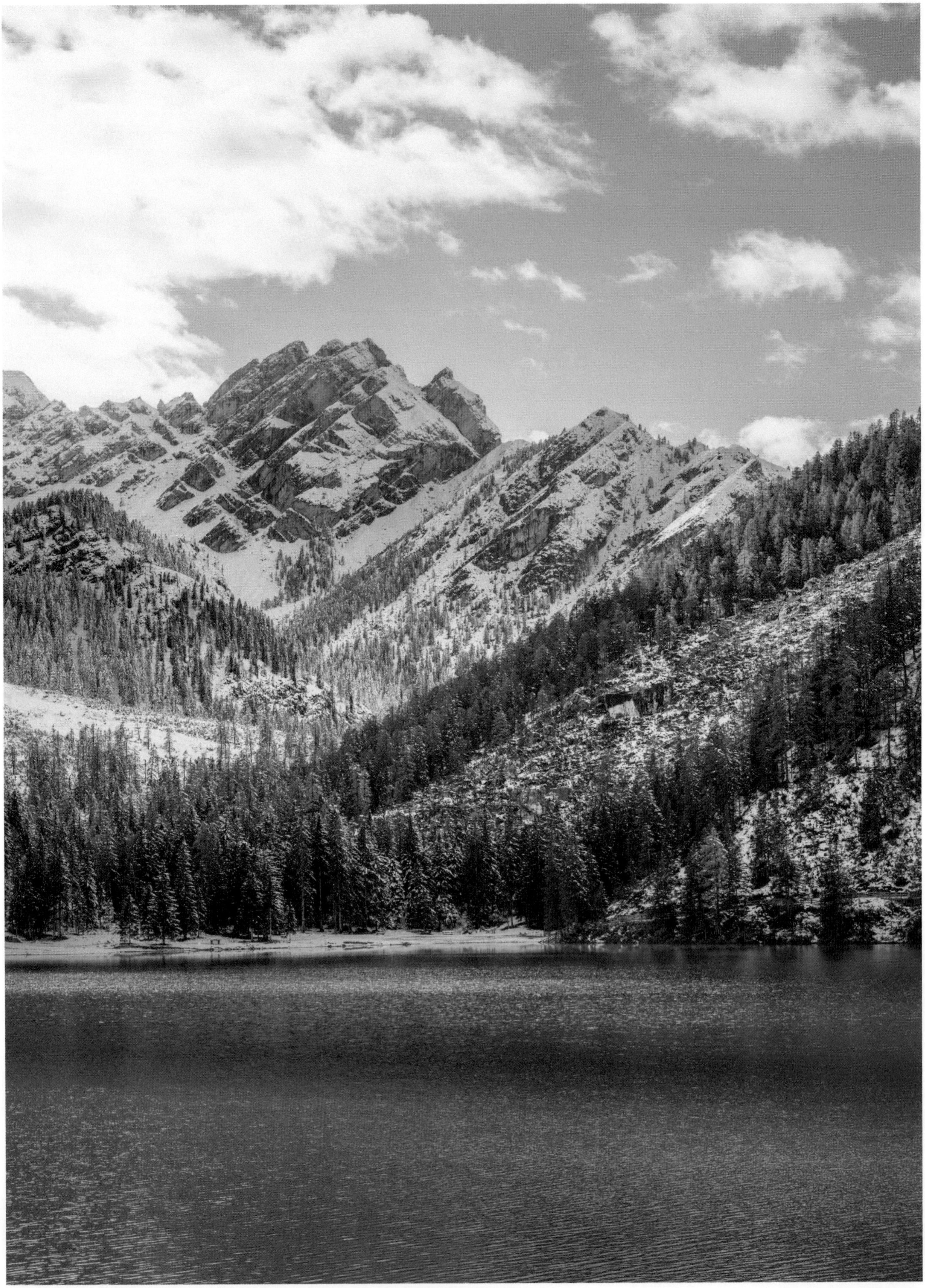

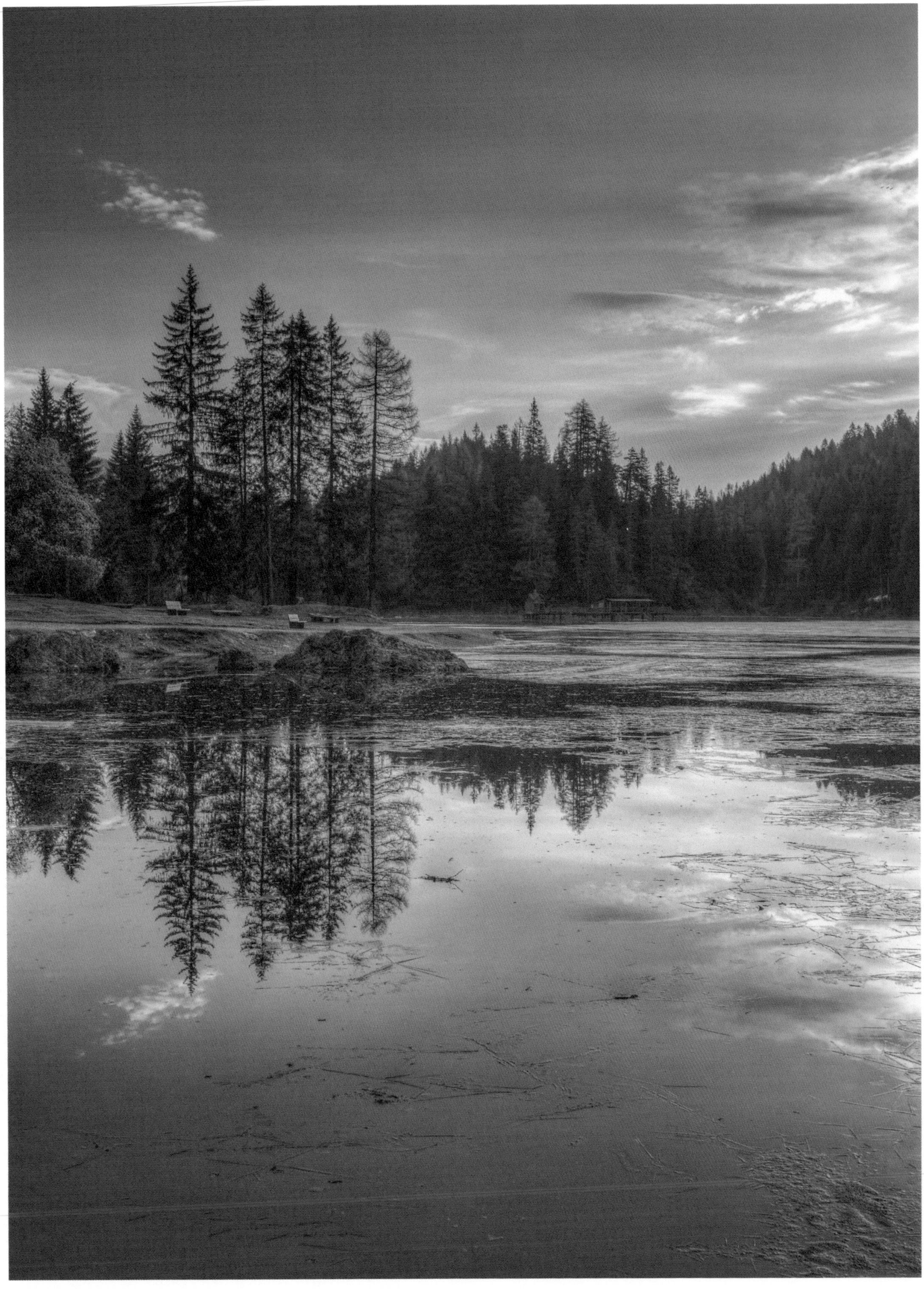

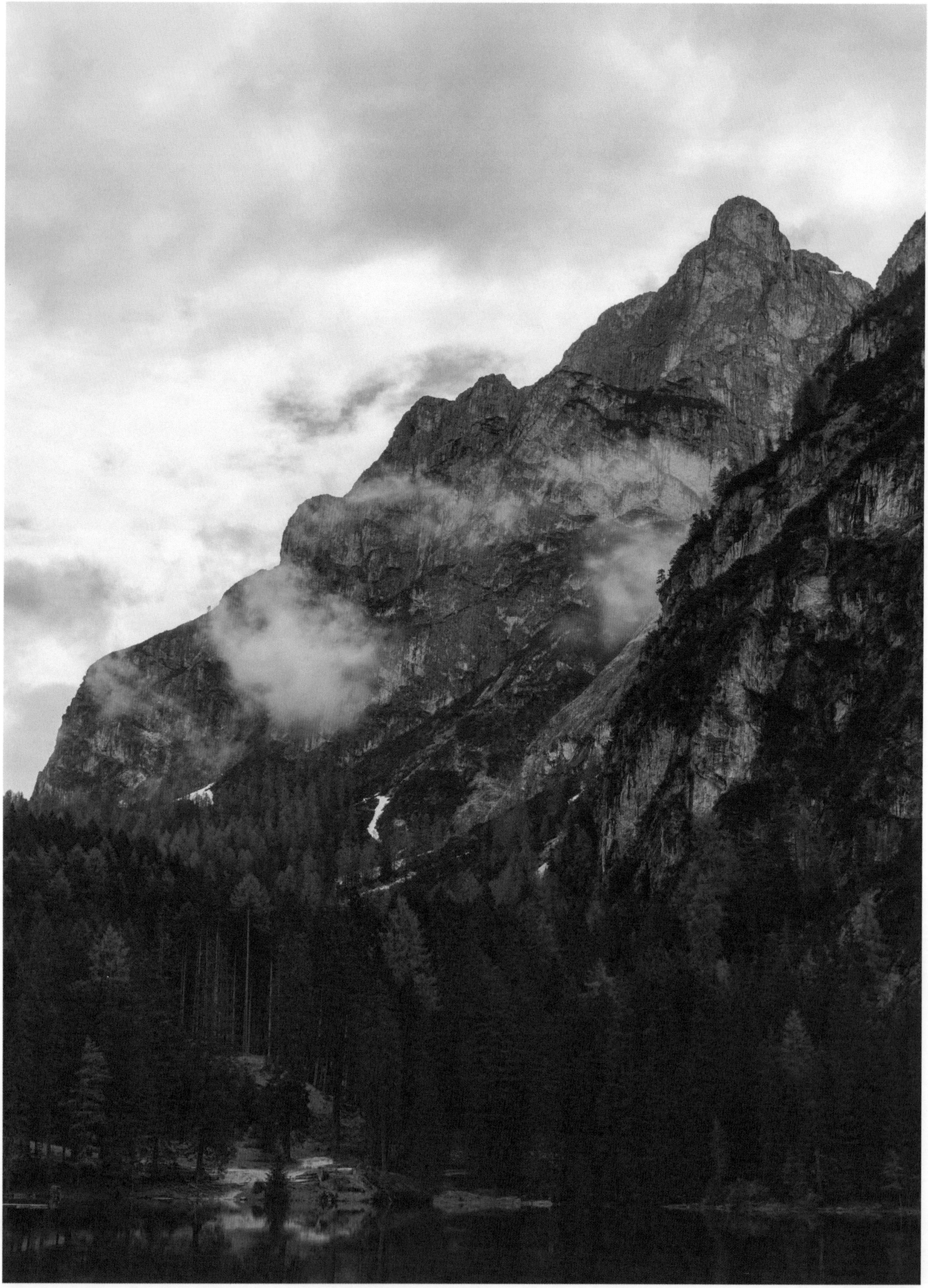

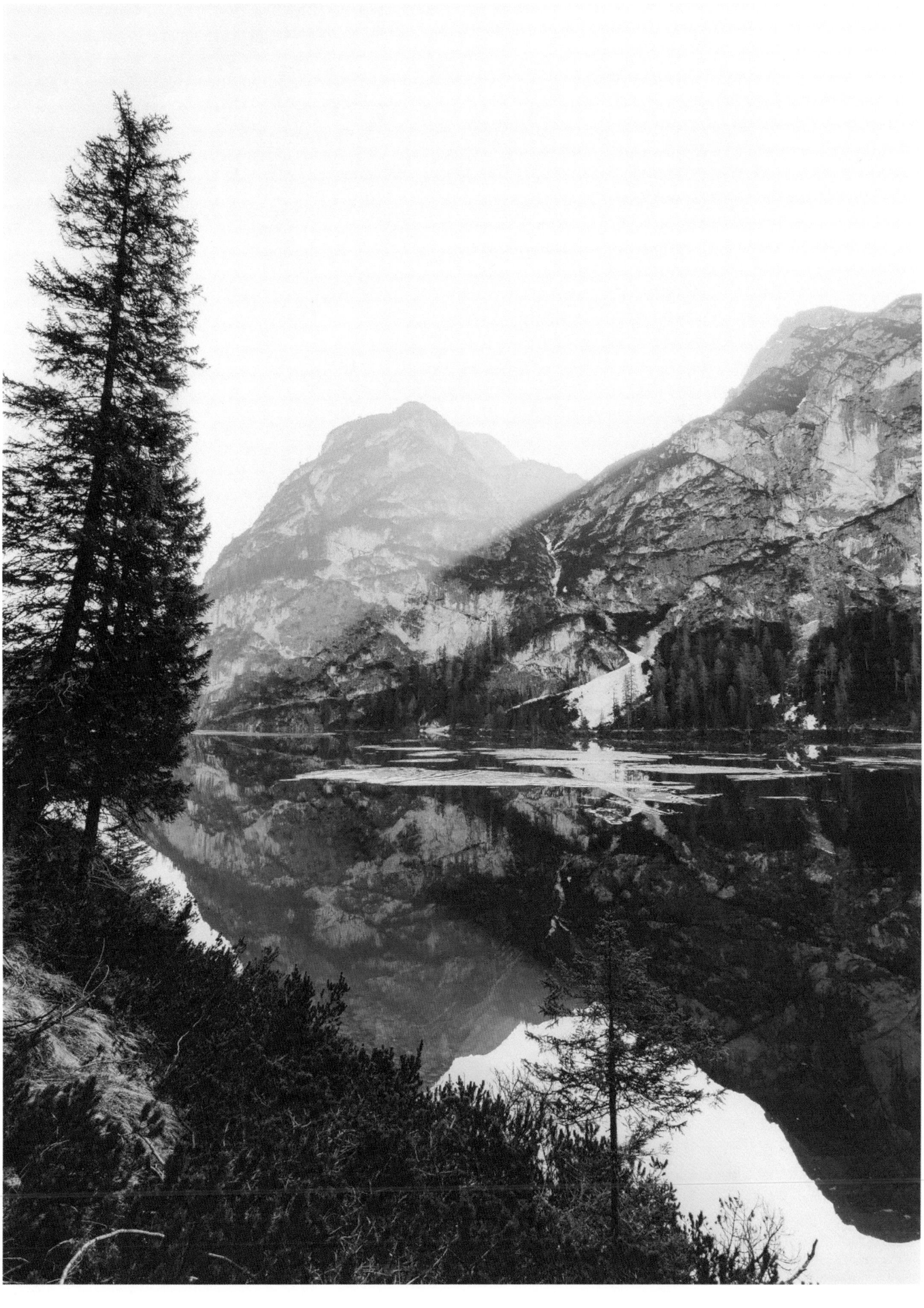

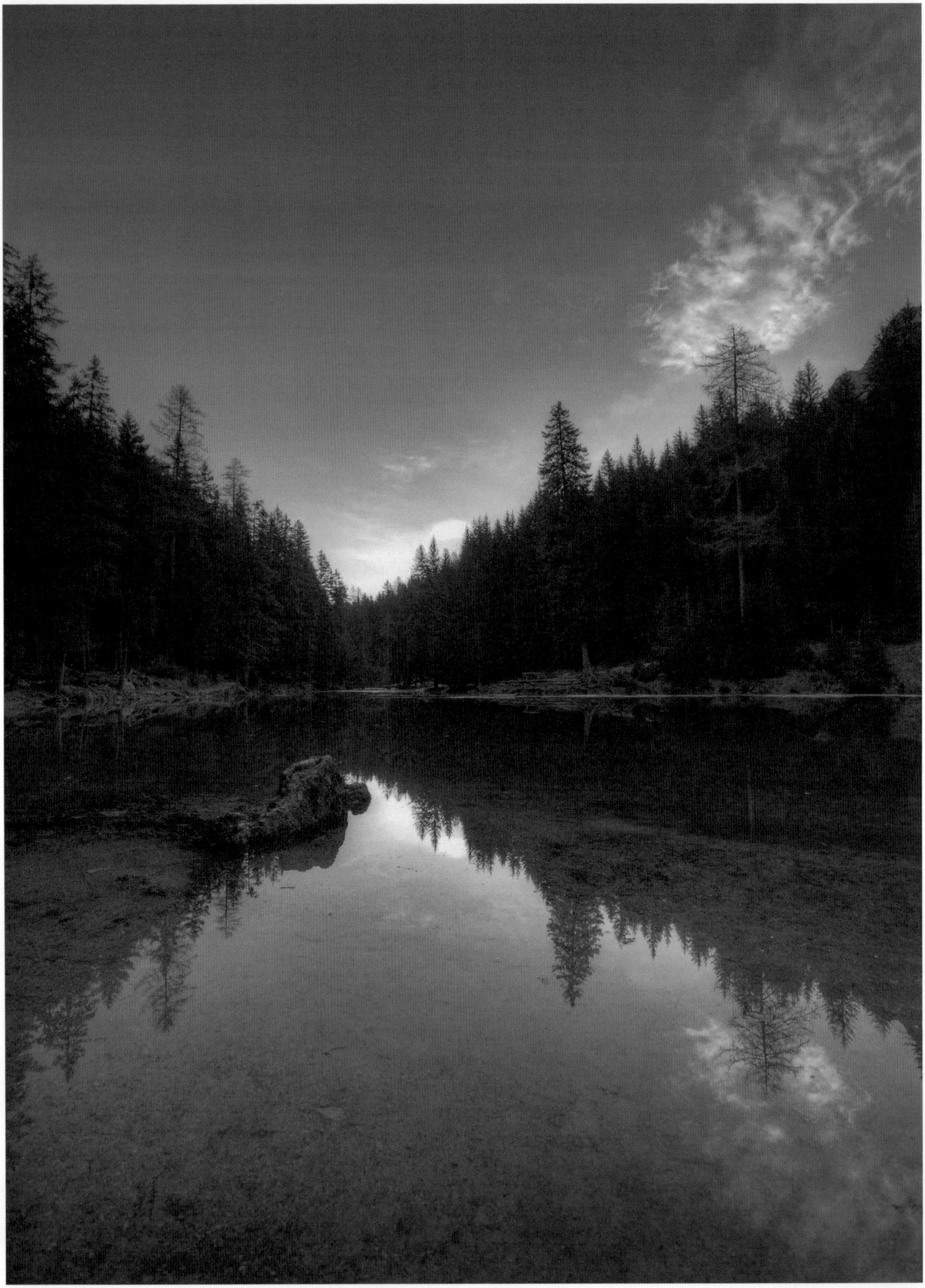

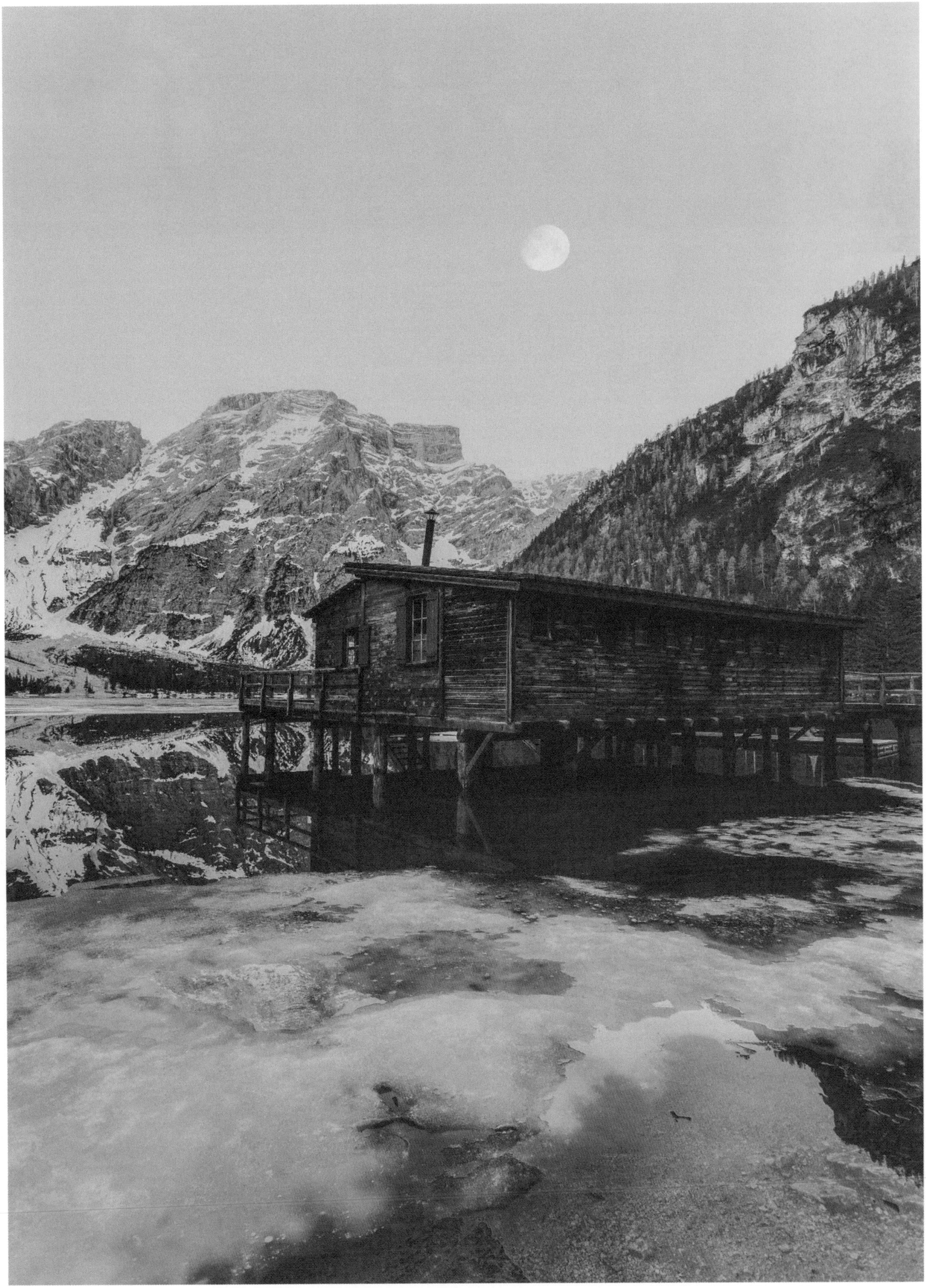

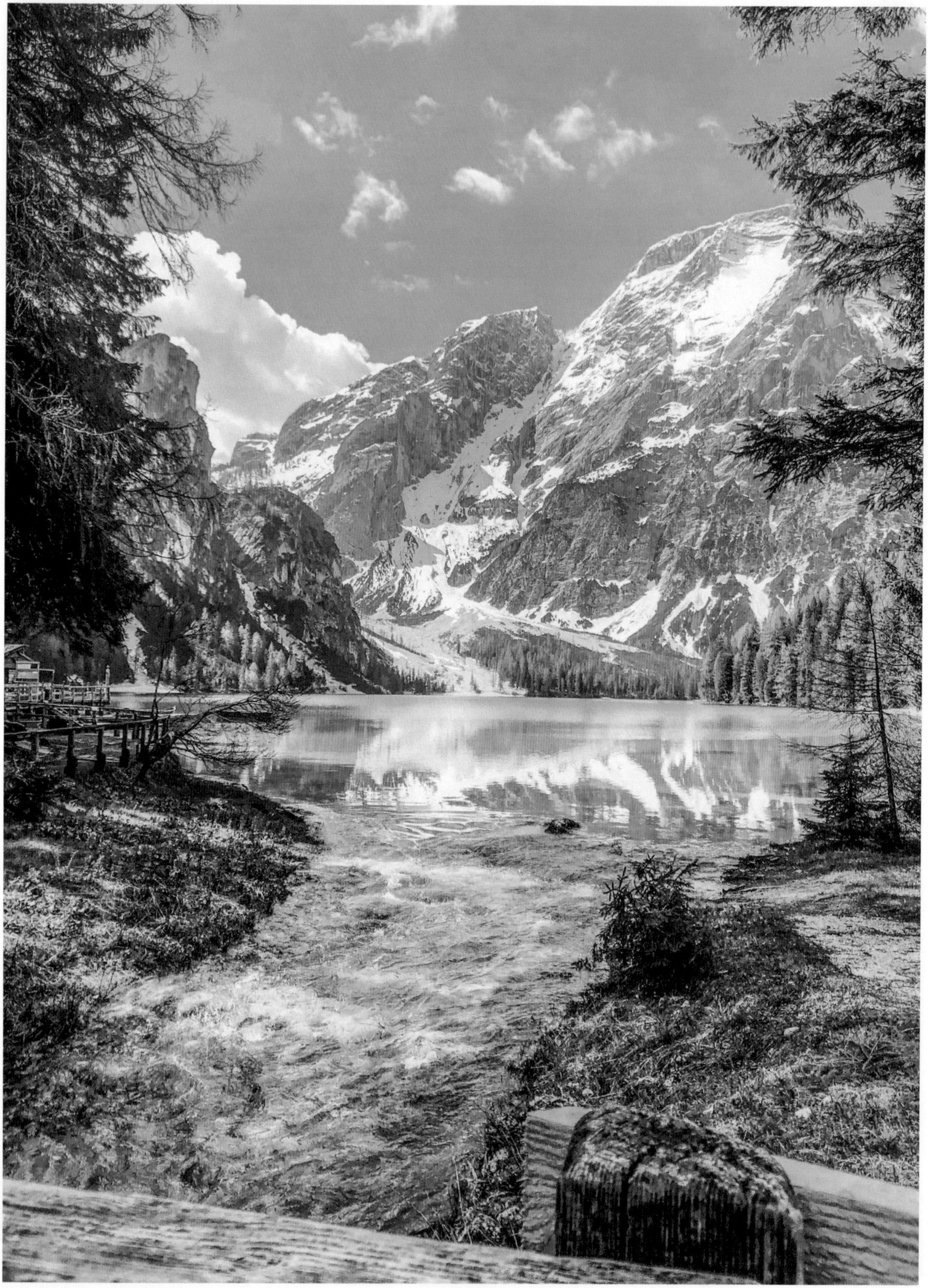

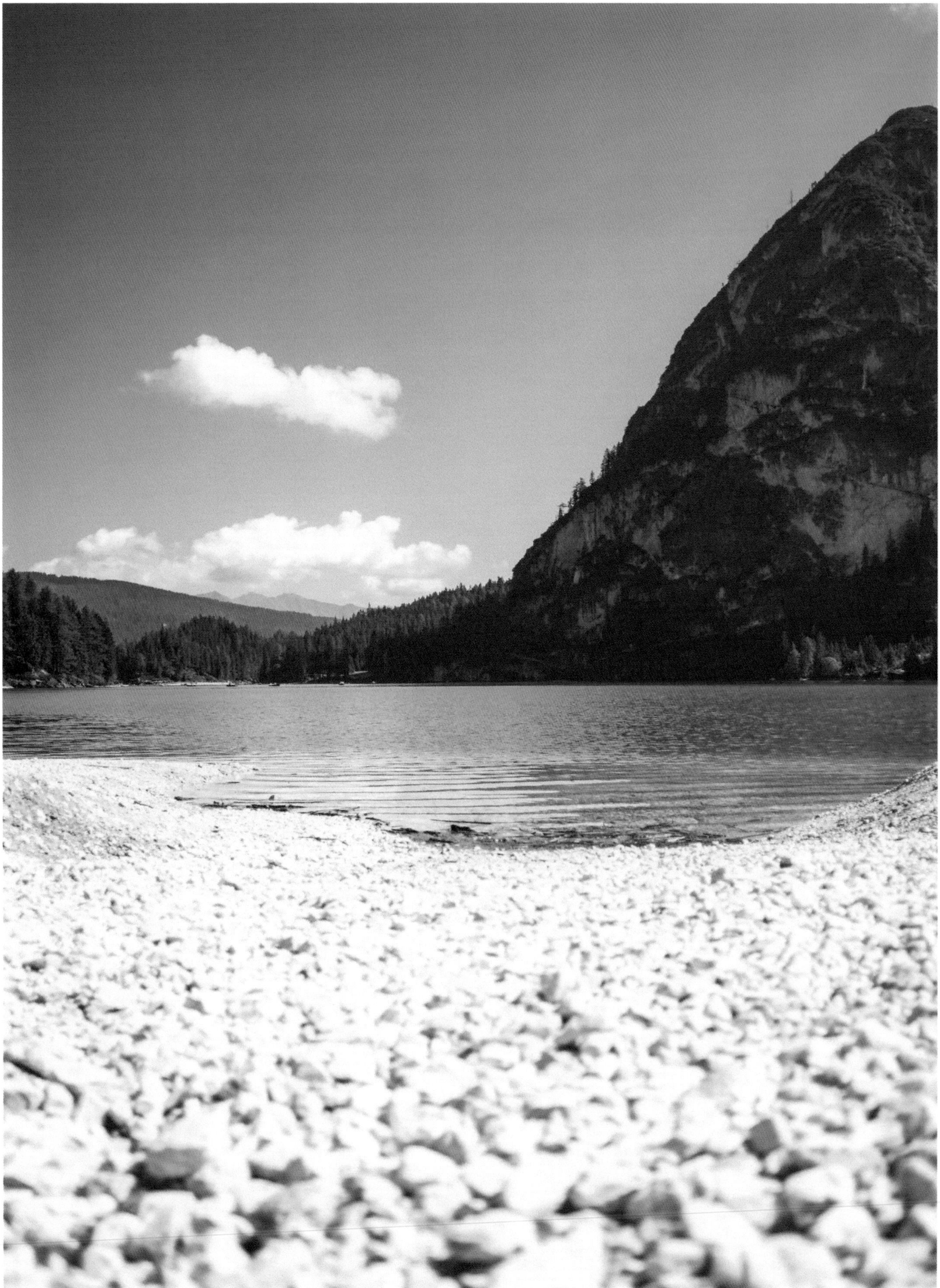

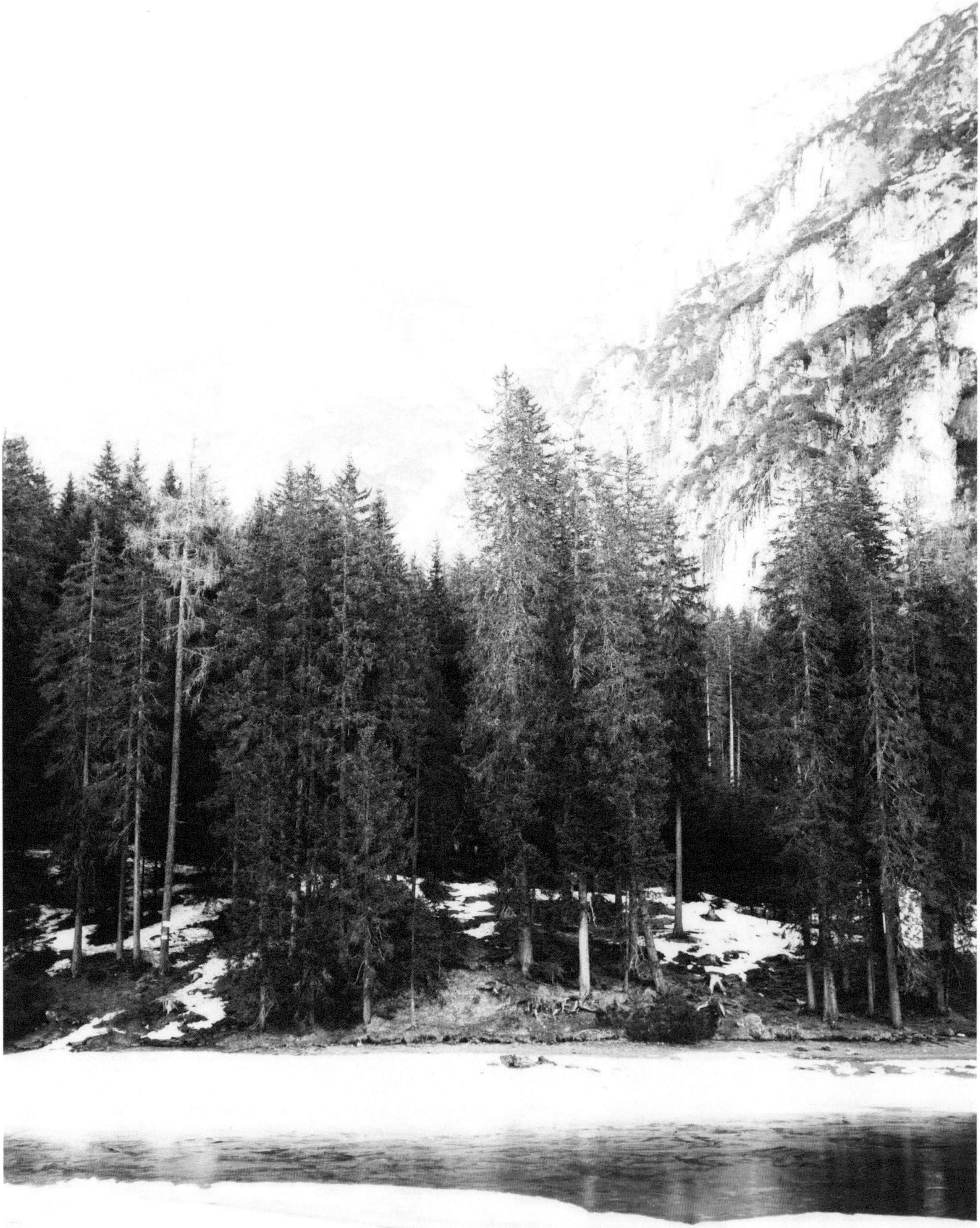

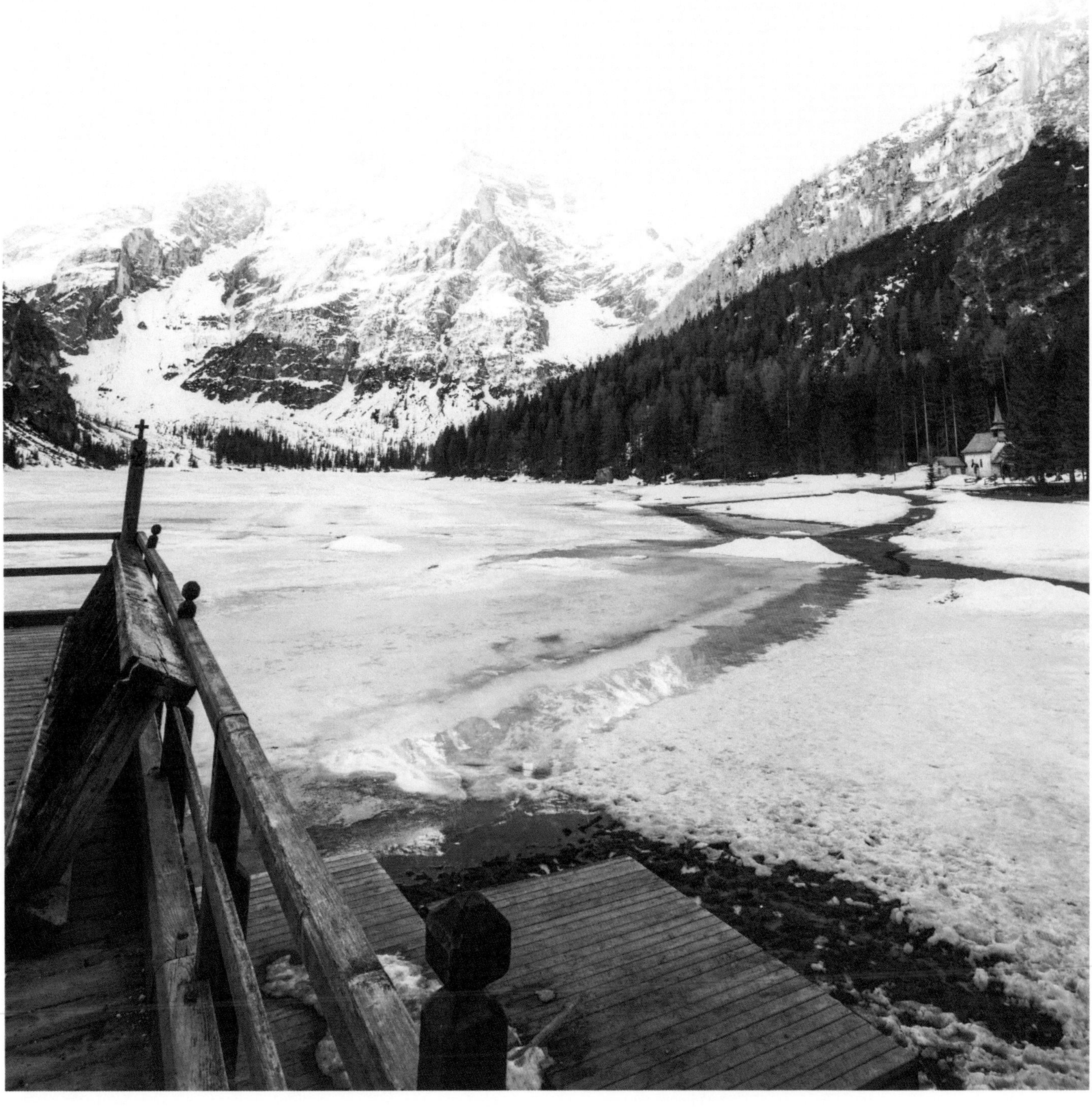

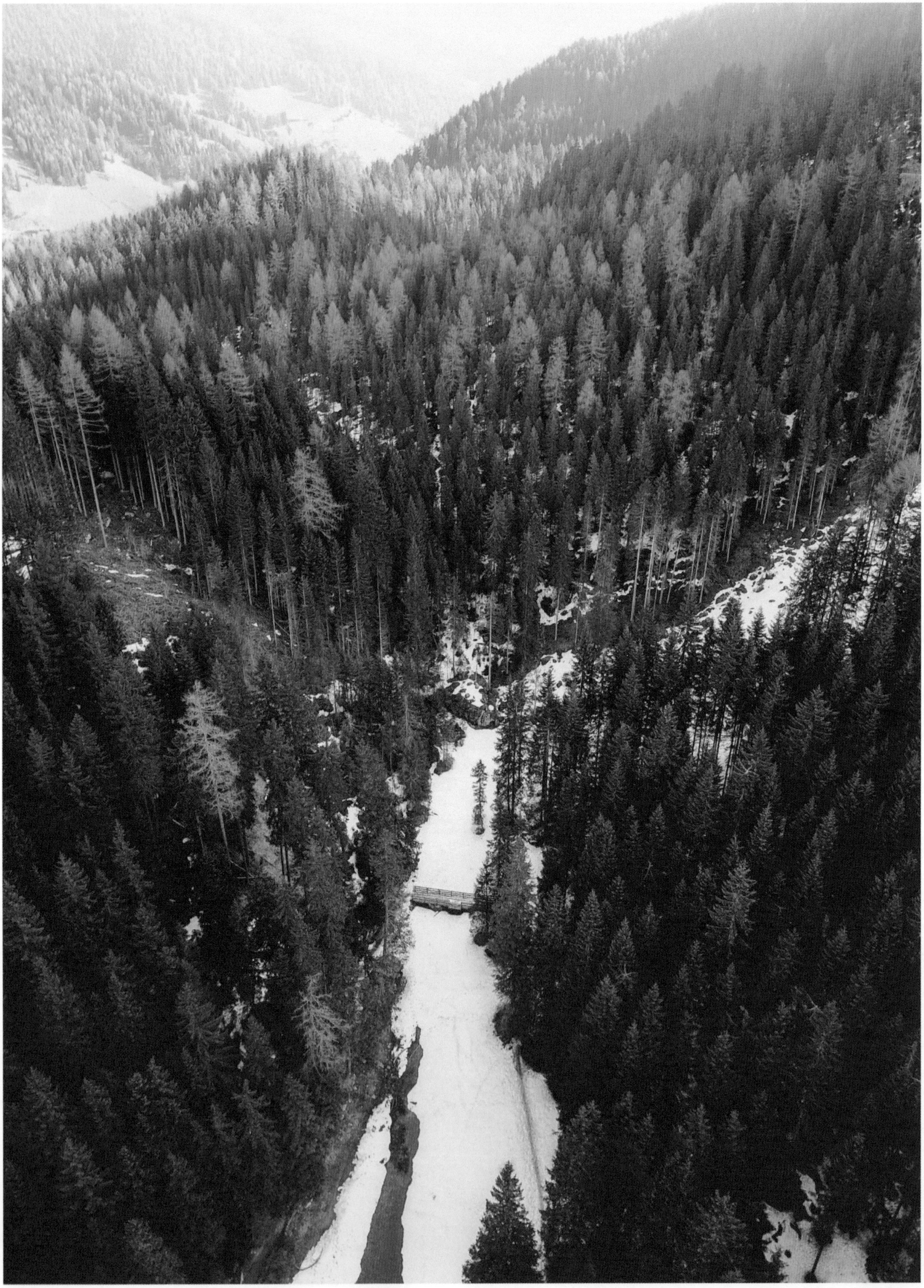

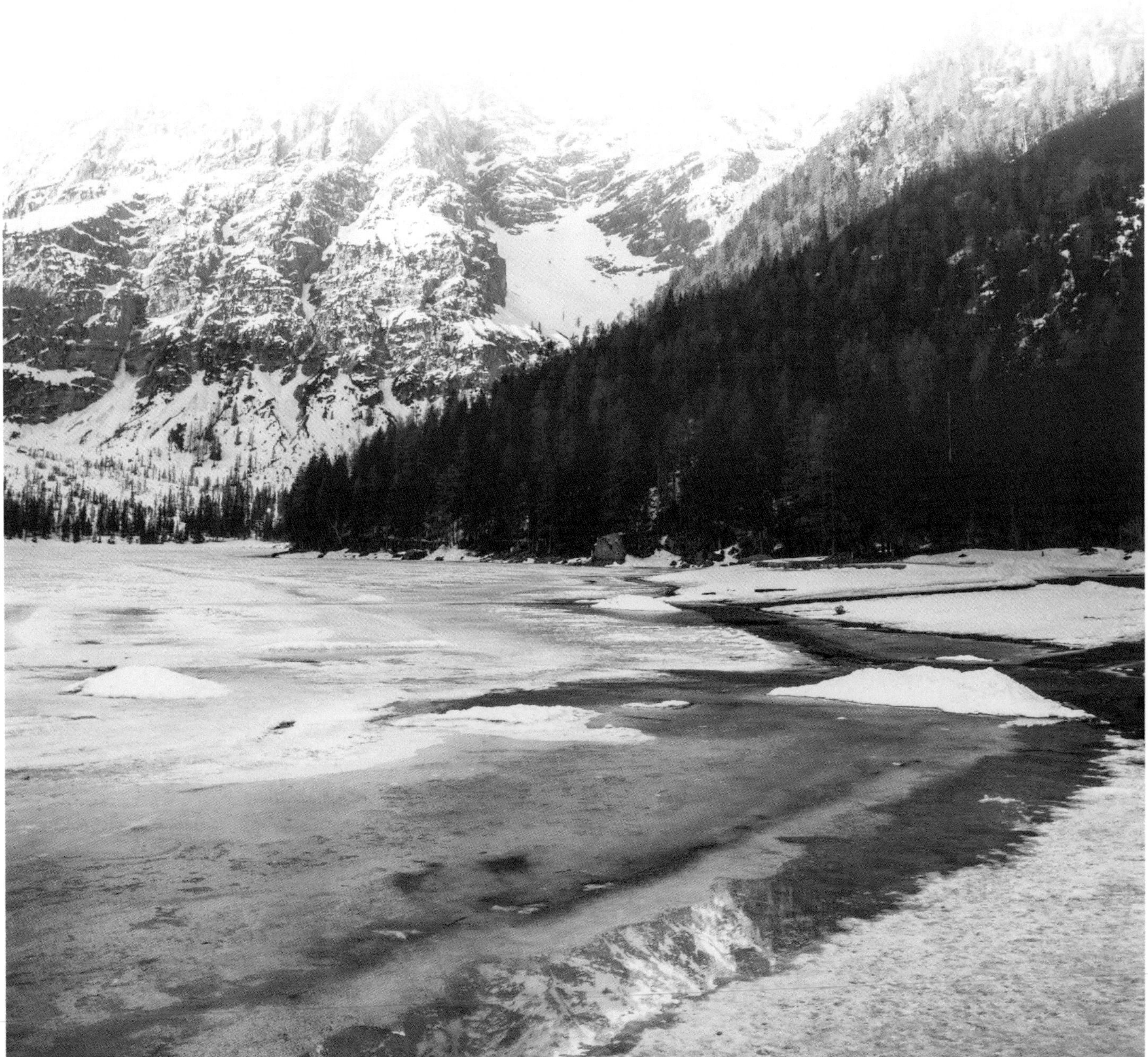

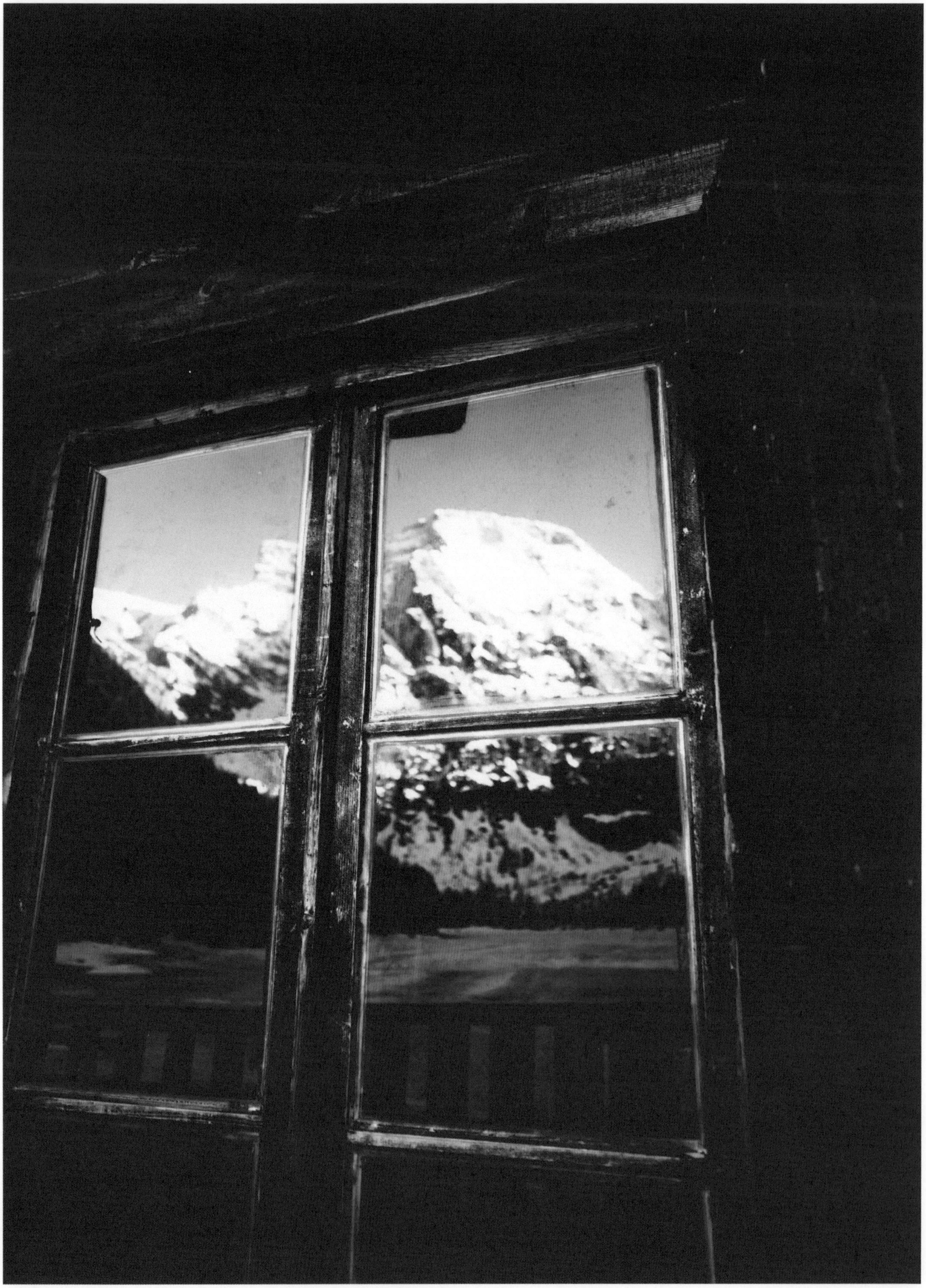

Printed in Great Britain
by Amazon

41637094R00025